TRANSCENDENT LIVING

*How to Transform your Life by Understanding
and Applying the Laws of Life!*

Isaac Heckman

Text Copyright © 2018 Isaac Heckman
All rights reserved.

Library of Congress Control Number: 2025918580
ISBN 979-8-9999582-8-0 (Hardcover)
ISBN 979-8-9999582-7-3 (Paperback)

No part of this book may be reproduced, stored in a retrieval system, or transmitted in any form or by any means—electronic, mechanical, photocopying, recording, or otherwise—without prior written permission of the author, except for brief quotations used in reviews or scholarly works.

Published by New Life Living Publishing
New York, New York

DEDICATED
TO THOSE WHO HAVE GONE BEFORE...

First and foremost, all glory goes to the Source of all light, life, law and blessings, without which nothing would be possible and through which all things are possible! Secondly, to my Father and Mother... my Father of blessed memory who always encouraged me, taught me to think beyond convention and gave me a general love for learning in all areas and always provided an extensive library for me to delve into books of antiquity and explore the unknown. And to my Mother who always sought to instill a deep spirituality, purity of heart and a connection to the Divine Source and who taught me to apply what I knew to be truth in every area of live no matter what the situation. I further dedicate this book to all who have gone before me who have sought to understand and live in harmony with the Divine Principles, have received further revelation and then helped preserve that wisdom down through the ages. Also to those dear friends who have faithfully encouraged me throughout the years in my pursuit of spiritual knowledge, encouraged me to teach these truths to others around the world and saw the vision of me writing this book to bless even more people with the restoration of this lost knowledge of the laws that govern every aspect of our existence. Their support has strengthened my continual search for deeper wisdom, knowledge and understanding—wisdom that has always inspired me to embody these principles in my own life and to inspire others toward lives of greater abundance, purpose, and meaning. May the insights within these pages, together with my spiritual teachings, humanitarian efforts, and commitment to facilitating health and wellness to all, serve as a blessing to all who earnestly seek to embrace the fullness and joy of a truly transcendent life!

CONTENTS

ACKNOWLEDGMENTS I

PART I: THE LAWS EXPLAINED 5

    CHAPTER ONE: THE 7 LAWS OF SPIRITUAL HEALTH AND BLESSINGS 7
        #1: The Law of Unity and Oneness *8*
        #2: The Law of Love *12*
        #3: The Law of Wisdom *16*
        #4: The Law of Power... the Power of Love *20*
        #5: The Law of Peace *24*
        #6: The Law of Creativity *27*
        #7: The Law of Eternal Life *31*
        Chapter Summary/Key Takeaways *34*

    CHAPTER TWO: THE 7 LAWS OF MIND AND MENTAL MASTERY 35
        #1: The Law of Cause and Effect *37*
        #2: The Law of Control *40*
        #3: The Law of Belief *43*
        #4: The Law of Expectation *46*
        #5: The Law of Attraction *49*
        #6: The Law of Correspondence *53*
        #7: The Law of Superconscious Activity *56*
        Chapter Summary/Key Takeaways *59*

    CHAPTER THREE: THE 7 LAWS OF EMOTION AND "HEART" HEALTH 61
        #1: The Law of Identity *63*
        #2: The Law of Situational Meaning *66*
        #3: The Law of Desire and Attachment *69*
        #4: The Law of Concern *72*
        #5: The Law of Apparent Reality *75*
        #6: The Law of Comparative Feeling *78*
        #7: The Law of Judgement and Guilt *81*
        Chapter Summary/Key Takeaways *84*

    CHAPTER FOUR: THE 7 LAWS OF PHYSICAL HEALTH 85
        #1: The Law of Nutrition *86*
        #2: The Law of Physical Movement *89*
        #3: The Law of Water *92*
        #4: The Law of Sunlight *95*
        #5: The Law of Temperance *98*
        #6: The Law of Air *101*
        #7: The Law of Regeneration through Rest *104*
        Chapter Summary/Key Takeaways *107*

CHAPTER FIVE: THE 7 LAWS OF RELATIONSHIP HEALTH 109
  #1: The Law of Equality 111
  #2: The Law of Mirror Reflection 114
  #3: The Law of Change 117
  #4: The Law of Mindfulness in the Present Moment 120
  #5: The Law of Choosing Happiness over "being Right"! 123
  #6: The Law of Feeding your Relationships 126
  #7: The Law of Communication 129
  Chapter Summary/Key Takeaways 132

CHAPTER SIX: THE 7 LAWS OF FINANCIAL HEALTH AND ATTRACTING ABUNDANCE 135
  #1: The Law of Realizing your Oneness with the Source of all Resource 136
  #2: The Law of Thinking, Believing & Feeling 139
  #3: The Law of Speaking only Good into Existence 142
  #4: The Law of Action 145
  #5: The Law of Receiving not for the Self alone but for the Greater Good 148
  #6: The Law of Righteousness and Wisdom 151
  #7: The Law of Gratitude 154
  Chapter Summary/Key Takeaways 156

CHAPTER SEVEN: THE 7 UNIVERSAL LAWS OF THE INVISIBLE REALM 159
  #1: The Law of Mentalism - "All is Mind" 161
  #2: The Law of Correspondence 164
  #3: The Law of Vibration 167
  #4: The Law of Polarity 170
  #5: The Law of Rhythm 173
  #6: The Law of Cause and Effect 176
  #7: The Law of Gender in all Things and on all Levels 179
  Chapter Summary/Key Takeaways 183

EPILOGUE/CONCLUSION 185

BIBLIOGRAPHY 187

ABOUT THE AUTHER 194

ACKNOWLEDGMENTS

With deep gratitude and humility, I offer thanks to all who have contributed to the unfolding of this work.

To the Creative Divine Source of all wisdom and truth—thank You for being the all pervading light that illuminates every path, the inspiration behind every word, and the silent guide behind every insight in these pages. This book is, first and foremost, a reflection of Your eternal love, presence, and law.

To the sages, prophets, mystics, and scholars—ancient and modern—who preserved and taught these sacred principles across generations, cultures, and traditions: your wisdom continues to ripple through time, awakening countless souls to higher understanding.

To the many awakened authors who sacrificed to convey the eternal truths and infinite accumulated wisdom of the past to lay the foundation for our current discussions on spiritual law, abundance, and consciousness—thank you for your courage to speak truth and share the vision.

To the teachers and mentors in my own life who modeled integrity, faith, and spiritual alignment—your example was more powerful than any lecture.

To my family and friends—thank you for your love, support, patience, and encouragement throughout this journey. Your belief in me has lifted my spirit and grounded my purpose.

To the readers of this book—thank you for your open heart and willingness to grow. May the principles within these pages empower you to live more freely, love more deeply, and create more consciously. Your journey matters, and your light is needed in the world.

Finally, to every seeker who dares to live a transcendent life—may you walk in truth, create in love, and flourish in harmony with the Divine laws that govern all things!

INTRODUCTION

Understanding the many Laws that Govern Life

Firstly, congratulations on taking the first step toward self-realization, self-development and restoration in attaining a truly Transcendent Life! **This book is about understanding Science and Spirituality in the pursuit of perfecting an Art... the Art of Living!**

We are all students in the lessons of life and it would do us well to know that the life that we cherish so dearly is governed by certain invisible laws that determine our health and wellness as well the intended bliss and blessings we are to meant to experience in every area of life including: Spiritually, Physically, Mentally, Emotionally, Relationally, Financially, and Universally. This book is a Self-Help book restoring this knowledge to those who will seek, and it will explain each of these forgotten laws to help each sincere student of life reclaim the blessings in every area of their life, so that they might experience a truly transcendent life experiencing the joys of transcendent spiritual heath, mental health, emotional health, healthy relationships and abundant financial wealth!

For most, we are unaware of the laws that govern everyday life and every aspect of our existence. We go through our days haphazardly planning and hoping for good things to come our way without realizing that we are either sowing into our lives blessings or the loss thereof through every thought, word and deed that is either in harmony with our applying the laws of life resulting in attracting blessings or those out of harmony due to ignorance and/or rebellion resulting in the loss of blessings.

Because mankind has largely lived in a self-preservation self-seeking mode, we have come to only believe in what we see in the physical realm and thus have forgotten that our true identity operates in the spiritual invisible realm... and that what manifests in the physical realm will always be the result of adherence to the laws in the spiritual unseen realm, and thus it is here that we err due to ignorance of these unseen laws and thus miss out on a truly Transcendent Life!

(The number one problem is that almost everyone has forgotten their true Divine identity and operating in that Divine identity in accordance with Divine laws is what Transcendent Living is all about! Just like a person's character determines how they will act and what they will attract, the Universe has laws that determine the cause and effect of all things manifested in the physical realm... This is the knowledge of how the Universe operates and how you can work within its laws to attract all things good! It cannot be understated how important it is for each person to know their true Divine identity because that will lead to fulfilling your true Divine purpose and thus changing your destiny!

People go through life thinking that they are this physical being, having an occasional spiritual experience, when in fact we are spiritual beings contained in a physical vessel having a physical experience through the physical senses. This unfortunately causes us to identify with our name, job, title, nationality, culture or religious creed that we were raised with, and it is just that which divides us from true Oneness with all things and blinds us to the power we have in the invisible realm to affect positive change through natural cause and effect. Be the change you wish to see in the world right now... There need be no delay in being what you desire for it is already within you. In the Divine essence which is the core of your true identity you have unlimited potential!)

It is not our parents nor teachers fault that they were not taught these laws... but throughout the ages, to the true seeker, these laws for transcendent living will always be revealed and then it is up to the diligence of the person to change their life to live in harmony with these laws to see blessings that are sure to be restored. It is my hope that this book be a collection of those laws for you as well as future generations in a clear and concise manner to reacquaint the reader with the source of health and abundance in every area of their life by revealing not only what these laws are but also how to live in harmony with them, thereby teaching the reader how to transform their life to transcend situation, space and time as the principles are applied!

Spiritual principles are not religious, nor does the reader need to be "religious". This book and these principles transcend ideology and religion and apply across culture and creed and will enable the reader to live more in harmony with the world family and all forms of life and thus is very unifying, transcending all the things that divide us and cause us to forget that we all come from the same source. (To break down the reader's preconceived religious paradigms I will use different general terms to convey the Source so as to bring us all together into a much closer union on this journey.) You will also find that each law is explained and confirmed by science for those of a more scientific mind.

In Hebrew and other ancient languages, the term "law" does not convey rules and restrictions but instruction in the principles that govern life. These laws stem from the very nature of the Source energy which operates only in the life-giving energy of selfless love, and thus all laws come from a loving source teaching us how to live and operate as selflessly loving beings...

appreciating and loving our Source as well as other life forms which come from the Source.

As mentioned above, there are seven different areas of our lives that are each governed by seven different laws that in total affect every aspect of our existence! The Parts to this book are divided by these "areas" and the chapters contain a clear and concise explanation of each of the seven laws pertaining to that "area" of our lives. These seven areas that affect every aspect of your being are your Spiritual, Physical, Mental, Emotional, Relational, Financial and then finally there are Universal laws that affect us and everything around us! **This is the beginning of that exciting journey relearning and restoring these principles which will bring everything back into harmony with health and happiness for you and those whom you share this knowledge with!**

This knowledge has been acquired from years of studying the common core principles taught by the world's greatest spiritual leaders throughout history. Wherever there is a principle seen in the universe and established by the great teachers, one will see that they all are confirming the same laws to live by. For Christians I have also included verses from scripture where applicable to show the deeper meanings of the apostles' teachings they learned from the principles of the ancient prophets. For Jews I have referenced Torah principles. For students of the eastern teachers, I have also included quotes from Gautama Buddha, Lao Tzu, and Confucius...

This book is meant to be a guide and for all who are on this journey and I, as author and guide, am here to facilitate your growth along the way. For more information, workshops and/or personal life-coaching, or to help us establish a Transcendent Living Center in your area please contact us info@transcendentliving.org

PART I: The Laws Explained

There is an ancient quote that says, "Happy are those that do the laws of life." But what are the "Laws of Life" and why are not taught them anymore? Obviously the wise of the ancient world knew and understood these Laws of Life and that *true Happiness comes from not just knowing and understanding, but also "doing" the laws*! It is my hope that the reader will hunger and thirst to apply the following understanding of the laws of life that they may find true happiness and health in every area of their life.

"None can be truly happy except he do the law" the Essenes wrote 2000 years ago and how true it is. For whatever law of life a man sows into, meaning invests time and energy into, that law will reap a great reward.

In fact, **the law is life!** The law is the living word of the living Divine source to living prophets (messengers) for living men. The living word is another way of saying the frequencies of these laws of life that permeate every aspect of our being and the visible and invisible universe! God originally wrote these laws not in the pages of books but *in your heart and in your spirit* and it is my hope that by re-learning these laws they will be written there once again for all to benefit and be blessed from!

The first lesson to convey is the importance of taking care of your heart and your spirit, by taking care of your mind and your vessel (body) which houses them, for if you desire that the laws of the living God benefit you, do not defile not your body and mind for the body is the temple of the spirit and the mind is the source of your transformation... therefore we must be diligent to purify the temple in mind and body for true transcendent health and happiness comes from a holistic approach of taking care of the mind, body and spirit!

The following explanations and examples of how to apply each of the Laws of Life is given with the intention that it is to be "lived out" and not simply for you to gain an "intellectual knowledge" of them. The amount of benefit depends directly on the amount of application and please know that God desires that you be blessed!

"Beloved, I wish above all things, that in all respects you may prosper and be in good health, just as your soul prospers." 3 John 1:2

This passage tells us 1) that it is God's desire for us to be blessed and in good health, and 2) that our health and blessings in the physical realm prosper "even as our Soul prospers" in the Spiritual realm! How important is that! This is a clue that attending to our Higher Self, i.e. Spirit and Soul health is paramount to everything else prospering and being in good health! And that is where we shall begin...

CHAPTER ONE:
The 7 Laws of Spiritual Health and Blessings

"The Divine Source's law is love and His gospel is peace." - *Essene wisdom from the Dead Sea Scrolls*

The Essene sons of Light 2000 years ago taught that **man's true identity** lies in the Spirit that created him and not in his body or circumstances. Mankind's spirit and consciousness comes from the Source Spirit that created him, often referred to in ancient times as "Heavenly Father", or in more modern times as "God", and a person's body (the vessel for the spirit) comes from the Earth. It was understood and taught that the Father's Spirit, like a seed, was placed in the womb of the earth, like a mother, thus the term Mother Earth came to be used even 2000 years ago. It was further understood that for Health and Happiness and Harmony in this life, one must live in accordance with both the **spiritual laws of Heavenly Father** and the **physical laws of Earthly Mother**. This first chapter explains those first **seven spiritual laws** of the Heavenly Father and how they relate to our spiritual health and understanding our true spiritual identity!

Law of Spiritual Health #1:
The Law of Oneness

Principle:
*All of creation—people, nature, spirit, and energy—is **interconnected**, flowing from one Divine Source*

The first of the Universal laws, "the Law of Oneness" stresses the interconnectedness of everything in this Universe. This includes people, things, thoughts, feelings, and actions. According to the law, all these are intertwined and any change in the status quo of one affects everything else.

This is hard for us to comprehend; to realize how even our thoughts and feelings will impact the lives of others around us. The logic behind this law is that we are all created from a single divine source and so, we are all part of the same. Physically we may seem separate to our naked eyes, but at some level beyond our understanding and senses, our beings are woven together mysteriously.

On a scientific quantum level, the Law of Oneness is seen and now proven that all life is interconnected—everything and everyone originates from and is part of a unified whole. On the quantum level, this truth is mirrored in the fabric of reality itself, as Quantum physics reveals that all particles emerge from a single unified field of energy. Through **quantum entanglement**, particles can become so deeply connected that the state of one instantly influences the other—no matter how far apart they are. This suggests that separation is an illusion; at the most fundamental level, everything is connected beyond time and space.

Additionally, the **observer effect** shows that consciousness and matter are intertwined: the act of observation affects outcomes. This means that our awareness is not separate from reality—it participates in shaping it.

Therefore, the Law of Oneness is not just spiritual wisdom—it is a quantum truth! **The more we live in awareness of this unity, treating others as extensions of ourselves, the more we harmonize with the very structure of the universe.**

Spiritually, we also come to realize over time that all things originate from a singular Source, (often referred to as "Heavenly Father") and this Source Consciousness is All in all and we are one with it! Furthermore, as we come from the Source of all things we can find transcendent joy in being one with all things! When Yeshua (Jesus) said, "I and my Father are one" he was disclosing to us the truth that our true Identity is the Spirit within us which comes from the eternal Source and thus is one with the Divine!

Thus, the illusion and deception lies in thinking that we are separate and so far from God who we are told is up in heaven when in fact he is within you, giving you life and consciousness, and giving you great creative power through your thoughts and speech as a co-Creator with the universal mind! This is why it is so important for us to transform our mind and speech, as the real "I" is Spirit and One with the Universal Eternal Mind. This attests to the ancient foundational principle that "God is One" meaning "Oneness" and "Unity" with all things... and since it is that Spirit that gives us life and consciousness, so are we! Thus, whenever I use the expression "I" or "I AM", I realize it is the full power of Love, Wisdom and Intelligence acting... and therefore I choose to connect and protect my mind in Harmony with the Spirit of Self-less love, for 'I AM' is the invisible guard, established, sustained, and maintained over my mind, my body, my home, my world, and my affairs... One and harmonious with all things through the great unifying law of love!

Application:

How to apply the Law of Oneness for a more Transcendent Life...

With this Transcendent realization, that I am a part of the Whole, I can honestly affirm (and you can too)...

*"I AM Light, I AM Love, I AM One with Source above,
I AM Compassionate, I AM Kind... it is all that's on my mind.
I AM Healthy, I AM Whole, I AM Spirit, I AM Soul."*

Mindfulness Practice:

"Unity Breath Meditation"

Take 5-10 minutes daily to practice the following:

1. Sit quietly and breathe deeply.
2. On the inhale, silently say: "I am connected to all that is."
3. On the exhale, say: "I send peace to all beings."
4. Visualize your heart energy expanding to include your family, community, humanity, and the entire planet. Feel the unity in your being.

Final Thought:

*The **Law of Oneness** teaches that all of creation—people, nature, spirit, and energy—is **interconnected**, flowing from one Divine Source. Though we appear separate as individuals, at the deepest level, **we are one essence**, united in spirit. This law reminds us that what we think, say, or do to others, we ultimately do to ourselves.*

*Remember: You are not a drop in the ocean—you are the ocean in a drop! When you live in harmony with the **Law of Oneness**, every thought becomes a prayer, every act becomes sacred, and every soul becomes your reflection. **To honor others is to honor yourself—and to love the world is to live as your highest self!***

Law of Spiritual Health #2:
The Law of Love

Principle:
"God is the conscious energy of Selfless Love"

The Law of Love is a core spiritual principle centered on unconditional love, unity, and compassion. It teaches that love is the highest law governing all life and that by expressing love toward the Heavenly Father, the Earthly Mother, and all living beings, one aligns with divine will. This law encourages selflessness, forgiveness, and service to others, viewing love as the force that connects and sustains all creation. Living by the Law of Love leads to inner peace, spiritual awakening, and deeper harmony with the universe.

All Source is Selfless Love and selfless love is the Source of Life. In the Bible, I John 4:8 says, "God is love" describing the very essence and nature of the Divine. Understanding the first law of Unity and that I am a part of God manifesting, I can proclaim, "If God is love, than I am love!"

When one is "enlightened in love" one will realize that real love is one of the paths to full spiritual liberation. This is because real love is giving and freeing and because freedom is the guide, the measure, and the ultimate goal of all things, real love includes those forms of love that are characterized by freedom... i.e. giving toward the well-being of all without any expectation of anything returned.

In seeking to cultivate a lifestyle and spirituality of love we need to be clear what we mean by real love, or more precisely, what real love looks like and what it does not look like: **Love is not mere sentiment or romanticism, nor is it something** dependent or elusive—difficult to grasp or sustain. Rather, it is our restless minds that so often interfere, limit, and encroach upon its true expression. Therefore, it is important to understand first the mind and its ways; otherwise we shall be caught in illusions, caught in words and sensations that have very little significance." Love that involves clinging, lust, confusion, neediness, fear, or grasping to self would be better termed imitation love as described by Dr. Greg Baer in his counselling to thousands around the world. Real love is Unconditional Love... In Real Love there is no disappointment, impatience, irritation, or anger. It is not dependent on what someone else is providing such as pleasure, prosperity, power, protection, or praise. (*Greg Baer, n.d.*)

At the quantum level, all matter and energy arise from a unified energy field—revealing an infinite, intelligent source vibrating with unlimited potential. This field is not cold or mechanical; many spiritual traditions and emerging scientific insights suggest it is *relational*, creative, and responsive to intention. The highest vibrational frequency that aligns with this field is **selfless love**—a force that transcends ego and seeks only to give, to uplift, and to unite.

Selfless love, unlike possessive or transactional emotions, mirrors the very structure of the quantum field: **non-dual, interconnected, and expansive**. Just as entangled particles act as one, selfless love dissolves the illusion of separation and reveals the unity behind all forms. It is the frequency that brings coherence, order, and harmony to the chaos of the quantum realm.

Thus, **selfless love is the original organizing principle of creation—and the vibration that aligns us with Source Itself!** When we love without condition, we synchronize with the quantum Source Field, becoming conduits for the creative power that gives birth to galaxies, life, and consciousness itself.

Application:

How to apply the Law of Love for a more Transcendent Life...

One of the most rewarding spiritual practices is to cultivate the ability to **bring love into all aspects of our life** and to all people we encounter. This entails learning how to include love's presence in thought, word and deed in every situation... even in the most difficult or painful of times.

To apply the Law of Selfless Love in one's life, one must give love freely without expecting anything in return. This involves practicing kindness, compassion, forgiveness, and empathy in all relationships. Selfless love means seeing the divine in others, serving those in need, and letting go of ego, judgment, and attachment. It calls for living from the heart—offering support, understanding, and care even in difficult moments. By making love the foundation of every action, one creates inner peace and helps uplift the world, embodying the true spirit of divine unity.

Mindfulness Practice:

"Self-check into Selflessness, giving and service"

1. Each day, ask yourself: *"Is this thought, word, or action coming from Love?"*

2. Let that question guide you into higher alignment.

3. Give generously, forgive freely, and speak kindly—not because you must, but because Love naturally flows through you.

Final Thought:

To live by the Law of Love is to live in God in God in You! When we love selflessly, we mirror the Source who is the original Giver. And in doing so, we become vessels of healing, harmony, and heavenly abundance—transformed by Love, and transforming the world through Love.

Law of Spiritual Health #3:
The Law of Wisdom

Principle:
"All wisdom comes from the Divine Source,
and is One with Him for ever...
Wisdom hath been created before all things,
and the understanding of prudence from everlasting.
The word of God most high is the fountain of wisdom;
and her ways are **everlasting laws.***" (Sirach 1:1,4-5)*

The Law of Wisdom teaches that true power comes not just from knowledge, but from using knowledge with discernment, understanding, and love. **Wisdom is the ability to see beyond surface appearances, make choices aligned with higher truth, and respond—not react—to life.** It is inner guidance applied to outer circumstances

The Law of Wisdom emphasizes the pursuit of divine knowledge and an inner understanding of one's Divine Identity as a path to spiritual enlightenment. According to this teaching, true wisdom comes from aligning the mind with the eternal truths of the Heavenly Father and observing the natural rhythms of the Earthly Mother. The ancient Essenes believed wisdom is not just intellectual but deeply spiritual—gained through meditation, reflection, and communion with higher realms. Living by the Law of Wisdom means seeking truth, practicing discernment, and using knowledge to foster harmony, healing, and growth in oneself and the world.

Knowing, Understanding and Applying Wisdom, also known as Superior Thought, is the key to success in any area of your life. From the remote ages of antiquity, a remarkable teaching has existed which is universal in its application and ageless in its wisdom. Traces of the teaching of connecting to Higher

Consciousness and applying Superior Thought to daily life has appeared in almost every country and religion as far back as ten thousand years. "For wisdom and power can come only from the love of God." (The Essene Gospel of Peace).

Wisdom it is said, was the first thing created. "The Lord *created* me [*wisdom*] at the beginning of his work, the *first* of his acts of long ago. –Prov. 8:22 [Quote also in Sirach 1]. This means that wisdom at it's core has to do with the nature of reality. But how do we come to know the reality of all things? Quantum physics has come to realize that everything is a part of a Higher Consciousness... the "Divine Mind" if you will... and we are already a part of the Quantum Consciousness in all things! All we have to do is stop, rest our lower "thinking mind" and connect to the pure Higher Consciousness that knows all things as they really are.

The Law of Wisdom on the Quantum Level is the ability to see the true nature of reality and act in alignment with it. On the quantum level, wisdom means understanding that reality is not fixed, separate, or purely material—but fluid, interconnected, and shaped by consciousness.

In quantum physics, particles exist in probabilities, not certainties, until observed. This means our awareness plays a role in shaping what becomes real. Wisdom, then, is the conscious choice to observe, intend, and act with clarity, purpose, and alignment with higher truth—not ego or illusion.

Quantum coherence—where systems operate in harmony—is a mirror of wisdom in action. It brings order to chaos, much like wise choices bring harmony to life. And just as entangled particles communicate beyond space and time, true wisdom transcends the limits of logic and taps into deeper, intuitive knowing that connects all things.

In essence, **the Law of Wisdom on the quantum level is about tuning into the underlying intelligence of the universe—and choosing to think, feel, and act in harmony with it.**

Application:

Applying the Law of Wisdom for a more Transcendent Life...

To apply the Law of Wisdom in daily life, one must seek truth, cultivate inner **clarity**, and live with **conscious awareness**. This involves regular **reflection, meditation, and communion with nature** and the Divine to deepen understanding.

It also means practicing **discernment**—making thoughtful choices based on insight rather than impulse—and learning from both experiences and silence.

Applying wisdom includes speaking and acting with integrity, being open to spiritual guidance, and using knowledge to bring peace, healing, and harmony to oneself and others. Ultimately, it is about aligning mind and spirit with higher truth.

To apply this law:

- Pause before acting or speaking, especially in emotionally charged situations.
- Ask yourself: *Is this response coming from fear or wisdom? From ego or truth?*
- Seek guidance from within—through prayer, meditation, or quiet reflection—before making important decisions.

Mindfulness Practice:

Try the *"Wisdom Pause."*

1. Once a day, when faced with a choice or challenge, take a few deep breaths and ask: *What would the wisest version of me do right now?*

2. Listen for the still, small voice of clarity within. Write down the guidance you receive and notice how following it impacts your peace and outcomes.

Over time, this practice builds inner strength and spiritual confidence—helping you live with clarity, grace, and purpose.

Final Thought:

Wisdom is the bridge between divine law and human action. When we embrace the Law of Wisdom, we live not just for success—but for significance. And through it, we begin to experience a transcendent life—one led by truth, marked by peace, and filled with the light of eternal understanding.

Law of Spiritual Health #4:
The Law of Power... *the Power of Love*

Principle:
Love is the Power and Love does not Force!

The Law of Power is rooted in the energy of Selfless Love, whereas "Force" (often mistaken for power) represents all thoughts and effort of the flesh and ego and selfish nature. All things which are possible via our own abilities and capabilities, in other words, our brute strength, making something happen against its natural will. **Power**, on the other hand, represents the wherewithal and strength accessed from Source, beyond the capabilities of mankind, based in unconditional love, all that is God, and the **power** of the universe.

A Scientist named David Hawkins once wrote, "**Power** arises with meaning and truth. It appeals to that we call nobility and equality, that which emboldens and builds up. **Force** always succumbs to **power** in the end. **Force** always creates a counterforce where **power** stands by itself and requires no outside energy and makes no demands. **Power** creates life and energy where **force** sucks it away...

Power is quiet and requires no explanation. **Force** is coercive and creates an automatic counterforce. This has great applicability for couples, parents and bosses. Standing on the side of truth, justice and all that sustains life is **power**. This is strength of its own merit. **Force** represents all that is negative and life destructive."

Thus, **Force** is the fundamental result of an interaction between two objects, while **power** is an expression of energy consumed over time (work), of which **force** is an element. Force and power can both be described and measured, but a **force** is an actual physical phenomenon, and **power** in itself is not.

On the quantum level, true power is not about control or domination—it is about alignment, resonance, and influence through coherence. The most powerful forces in quantum physics—like entanglement and the zero-point field—operate silently, invisibly, yet profoundly. They do not force outcomes; they shape reality through presence and connection.

Likewise, **love is the highest form of power because it does not force—it attracts, harmonizes, and transforms.** In quantum terms, love creates coherence: it brings scattered energies into alignment, just as coherent light (like a laser) has far more impact than unfocused light.

Force, by contrast, disrupts and fragments. It works against the field. But love—as quantum power—works *with* the field, flowing in harmony with the universal design. It doesn't manipulate; it magnetizes. It doesn't dominate; it resonates.

Thus, **the Law of Power at the quantum level teaches that true power is gentle, aligned, and irresistible—because it flows from love, not control.**

From a spiritual perspective, Rabbi Shaul wrote 2000 years ago to those spiritually awakening in Ephesus, "be strong in the Source and in the strength of His power." (Eph. 6:10) and then to the Colossians he wrote, "We continually ask God to fill you with the **Da'at knowledge** of His will through all the **Chokmah wisdom** and **Binah understanding** that His Spirit gives, so that you may live a life worthy of the Source and please Him in every way: bearing fruit (from the Spiritual "Etz Chaim" Tree of Life attributes of God) in every good work, growing in the **knowledge** of God, *being strengthened with all Power* (*toqeph* תֹּקֶף - *power, strength, energy*) according to his glorious might so that you may have great endurance and patience, and giving joyful thanks to the Father, who has qualified you to share in the inheritance of his holy people in the kingdom of light. (Col. 1:9-12)

2 Peter 1:3 says, "**Divine power** has granted to us all things that pertain to life and godliness, through the knowledge of Him who called us to His own glory and excellence." Thus, we must learn to not rest in the wisdom of men but in the power of God and live by the wisdom of His character of Selfless love which is the power and never forces... even though the world may not recognize it yet... For the wisdom of God is foolishness to man.

To apply the Law of Power in one's life, one must cultivate inner strength through spiritual discipline, self-control, and alignment with divine and natural laws. True power is developed by mastering one's thoughts, emotions, and actions—choosing responses rooted in peace, love, and purpose rather than fear or ego. Regular practices like meditation, prayer, and time in nature help connect to the universal source of energy. This inner power should be used not for control over others, but for healing, service, and creating positive change. It is the strength to live authentically and serve a higher good.

Application:

Applying the Law of Power (Not Force) for a more Transcendent Life...

> The Law of Power teaches that true strength flows from inner alignment, authenticity, and calm authority—not from control, coercion, or aggression. Power is rooted in spiritual confidence and clarity; it influences through presence and integrity, not pressure. Force may create short-term results, but power creates lasting transformation.

To apply this law:

- Let go of the need to dominate or push outcomes. Instead, align your thoughts, words, and actions with truth and purpose.
- Trust that calm conviction and inner certainty are more effective than striving or struggle.
- Focus on being rather than forcing—radiating confidence, compassion, and grounded intention.

Mindfulness Practice:

Try the *"Centered Presence Exercise."*

1. Each morning, spend 2–5 minutes in stillness. Breathe deeply and affirm: *"My power comes from within. I act with calm confidence and trust the flow of life."*

2. Then, carry that calm into your interactions throughout the day. Notice how others respond to your quiet strength.

Final Thought:

Practicing true power allows you to influence your world with grace, not resistance—leading from within rather than reacting from fear.

Law of Spiritual Health #5:
The Law of Peace

Principle:
"As far as possible be at Peace with all men."

The Law of Peace teaches that true peace begins within and extends outward to all creation. It is a state of harmony with oneself, others, nature, and the Divine. Peace is not merely the absence of conflict, but a deep spiritual balance rooted in love, wisdom, and truth. To live by this law is to cultivate inner stillness, practice forgiveness, avoid harm, and foster unity in all relationships. Peace is seen as both a daily practice and a sacred goal, leading to wholeness, healing, and alignment with the eternal.

If more would learn to abide by these laws, the world would be a better place and there would be peace and happiness... in fact when anyone begins to realize even the first law in regards to their true divine identity and unity with Source, they will always be at peace and harmony and unity with all things... as all things come from that same Source!

On the quantum level, everything is energy—vibrating fields of potential influenced by thought, emotion, and intention. Inner peace is not just a psychological state; it is a specific, **stable and coherent frequency** that aligns with the natural harmony of the quantum field.

When you cultivate inner peace—through presence, surrender, or meditation—you reduce internal noise and resistance. This mirrors **quantum coherence**, where particles align in perfect harmony, allowing for maximum efficiency and flow. Inner peace brings your personal field into resonance with the universal field, allowing energy, intuition, and even outcomes to shift effortlessly.

In contrast, stress, fear, and chaos create incoherence, disrupting your connection with the quantum field and limiting your ability to manifest or perceive clearly.

Therefore, the Law of Inner Peace reveals a truth on the quantum level: when your inner state is calm and coherent, you become a clear channel through which the intelligence of the universe can flow. Peace is not passive—it is quantum power in its purest, most receptive form.

To apply the Law of Peace in one's life, one must cultivate inner calm, live with compassion, and seek harmony in all relationships. This begins with practices like meditation, mindfulness, and honest self-reflection to quiet the mind and heal emotional conflicts. It also means responding to others with kindness, resolving disagreements peacefully, and avoiding harm in thought, word, and deed. By living in alignment with truth, love, and balance, one becomes a source of peace for the world. True peace flows from within and radiates outward, uniting all life in harmony.

Application:

Applying the Law of Peace for a more Transcendent Life...

> The Law of Peace teaches that inner calm is the foundation for true clarity, strength, and well-being. When you cultivate peace within, you become less reactive to external chaos and more anchored in your higher self. Peace is not the absence of problems, but the presence of spiritual alignment and trust in divine order.

To apply this law:

- Make inner peace your priority—before solving problems, responding to others, or making decisions.
- Choose thoughts, environments, and actions that nurture calm and centeredness.
- Release the need to control everything; instead, surrender to a higher flow and trust that all is working for your good.

Mindfulness Practice:

Use the *"Peace Alignment Pause."*

1. Several times a day, close your eyes, take three slow, deep breaths, and silently affirm: *"I am centered in peace. I choose stillness over struggle."*

2. Let that feeling wash over you before continuing with your day.

Final Thought:

By regularly returning to peace, you train your mind and spirit to operate from a place of harmony, allowing you to respond to life with clarity, compassion, and strength.

Law of Spiritual Health #6:
The Law of Creativity

Principle:
*Our Spirit is creative by nature
and is most fulfilled when it is creating.*

We were created in the image of the Divine Creator and thus are co-creators. God thinks or conceives of something and then speaks it into existence. The Bible says God first conceived of making man in His image and then spoke Creation into existence and this is a fundamental principle for how we manifest and create things as well.

The Law of Creative Action teaches that humans are co-creators with the Divine, endowed with the ability to shape their reality through thought, word, and deed. This law emphasizes conscious, purposeful action aligned with spiritual truth and natural harmony. By channeling divine inspiration and living in tune with the laws of the Heavenly Father and Earthly Mother, individuals can manifest beauty, healing, and transformation in the world. Creative Action is seen as a sacred expression of inner truth, and when guided by love and wisdom, it becomes a powerful force for personal and collective evolution.

This law of Creativity tells us that we need to align our actions with our thoughts and feelings. In other words, we must connect our thoughts and visions with our emotions as well as inspired actions. Only this can lead to manifestation. (We will elaborate more on this in later chapters with the Laws of Mental Mastery and the Laws of the Emotional Heart Health). Remember that this law works most powerfully when used for the greater good as the Creative Source energy is selfless and giving by nature.

At the quantum level, reality is not fixed—it's a field of infinite potential, waiting to take form based on observation, intention, and vibration. This mirrors the nature of the human spirit: **inherently creative, designed to shape and express reality through thought, emotion, and inspired action.**

Our spirit thrives when it is creating, because creation is how we participate in the unfolding of the universe. Just as a quantum particle doesn't exist in a definite state until observed, our ideas and visions don't become real until we *focus*, imagine, and bring them forth. This is **creation at the quantum level—turning possibility into form through conscious engagement.**

Creativity brings our inner world into resonance with the universal field. When we create from the spirit—with love, purpose, and authenticity—we're not just making art or solving problems; we're aligning with the **fundamental process of creation itself.**

Thus, the Law of Creativity teaches that to create is to fulfill our deepest spiritual design—and in doing so, we activate the same quantum power that shaped the stars.

To apply the Law of Action in one's life, one must act with intention, awareness, and alignment with divine purpose. This means transforming inner guidance, love, and wisdom into concrete deeds that serve the greater good. Every action—no matter how small—should reflect truth, harmony, and compassion. Instead of reacting impulsively, one chooses mindful, purposeful actions that support growth, healing, and unity. Creative expression, service to others, and living one's values in daily life are all ways to honor this law. Right action turns spiritual understanding into real-world impact.

Application:

Applying the Law of Creative Action for a more Transcendent Life...

The Law of Creative Action teaches that ideas, dreams, and intentions only become reality when combined with purposeful action. Thought is the blueprint, but action is the builder. When you align inspired thought with consistent movement, you activate the creative process and begin to shape your world with intention.

To apply this law:

- Don't wait for perfect conditions—take small, aligned steps toward your vision.
- Trust your inner guidance and act on inspired ideas quickly, before doubt sets in.
- See every action, no matter how small, as a seed planted toward your desired outcome.

Mindfulness Practice:

Try the *"Daily Inspired Action Step."*

1. Each morning, ask yourself: *What one action can I take today that moves me closer to my goal?*

2. Write it down and commit to doing it, no matter how simple. Over time, these daily steps build momentum and turn ideas into reality.

Final Thought:

Living by the law of Creative action empowers you to co-create your life—by thinking with intention and acting with faith.

Law of Spiritual Health #7:
The Law of Eternal Life

Principle:
Eternal life is intended for my spirit consciousness...

"And this is the promise God promised us, even the life eternal." - 1 Jn 2:25

If we connect with Selfless source and let the Spirit of Selfless Love flow through our every thought, word, and deed we metaphorically "walk with God" and experience Oneness with the Eternal One!

The Law of Eternal Life is a spiritual teaching emphasizes harmony with divine, natural, and personal laws as the path to eternal life. It teaches that eternal life is not just connected to this body, nor simply an afterlife promise, but a state of being achieved through purity of body, mind, and spirit. Central to this belief is living in accordance with the laws of the Heavenly Father (spiritual truth) and the Earthly Mother (nature), practicing compassion, inner peace, and daily communion with divine forces to attain unity with the eternal.

On the quantum level, energy cannot be created or destroyed—it only transforms. This mirrors the truth of our being: we are not merely physical bodies, but **eternal energy, consciousness**, and extensions of the infinite Source field that gives rise to all existence.

Just as quantum particles exist as waveforms of potential before collapsing into form, our true essence exists beyond time and space, woven into the quantum field that holds all possibilities. The body may change, but the consciousness—the *observer*, the *awareness*—continues, because it is not bound by matter. It is part of what ancient wisdom and modern physics both point to: **a unified, intelligent, eternal field.**

The Law of Eternal Life reveals that our soul or spirit is not separate from Source, but an ongoing **expression** of it—like a wave in the ocean. We may take form, dissolve, and rise again in new ways, but our essence remains part of the whole.

Thus, on the quantum level, Eternal Life is not only possible—it is natural. We are energy, consciousness, and love—forever connected, forever evolving, never-ending.

To apply the Law of Eternal Life in one's life, one must live in harmony with the divine, nature, and the inner self. This involves nurturing the body through natural living, the mind through truth and wisdom, and the spirit through love and communion with the Heavenly Father and Earthly Mother. Eternal life is not only a future state but a present way of being—achieved by living purely, peacefully, and purposefully. Daily practices such as meditation, gratitude, service, and connection with nature help align with eternal principles, allowing one to experience the timeless flow of life here and now.

Application:

Applying the Law of Eternal Life for a more Transcendent Life...

>The Law of Eternal Life teaches that your true essence is spiritual, infinite, and eternal—beyond the limits of the physical body or temporary conditions. When you live from the awareness of your divine, eternal nature, fear loses its grip, and you begin to see life through the lens of peace, purpose, and higher truth.

To apply this law:

- Shift your identity from a limited, mortal self to your higher, eternal self—spirit, soul, consciousness.
- Let go of fear-based thinking and embrace decisions rooted in love, truth, and spiritual vision.
- See challenges not as threats, but as opportunities for soul growth and eternal learning.

Mindfulness Practice:

Use the *"Eternal Self Reflection."*

1. Each day, spend a few quiet moments affirming: *"I am not just a body—I am eternal spirit, one with divine life."*

2. Reflect on your choices and thoughts from this higher perspective. Ask: *Am I acting from fear, or from the eternal truth of who I am?*

Final Thought:

Living from this Law of Eternal Life brings lasting peace, dissolves fear of loss or death, and inspires you to live with deeper meaning, love, and courage!

Chapter Summary/Key Takeaways

In summary, you are Spirit, you are love, you are one with Source above! In Overview, the 7 Spiritual Laws keep you connected to your True Higher Self and all the Transcendence that comes with that, operating from a Higher level of Consciousness and Awareness helping you live according to Creative Law and enabling you to transcend the various situations of the physical world and live your best life and highest purpose!

1) **One Unity:** All things come from the Source and I am one with it.
2) **Love:** All Source is Selfless Love and selfless love is the Source of Life
3) **Wisdom:** I have access to Knowing, Understanding and Applying Superior Thought
4) **Power:** The Source of true Power comes with knowing your connection with Source and is not to be confused with Force, or Manipulation of Someone else's free will.
5) **Peace:** As far as possible be at Peace with all men. To find peace, let go of all external chaos and internal reactions.
6) **Creativity:** Our Spirit is creative by nature and we are most fulfilled when creating things for the good of others.
7) **Eternal life:** The Law of Eternal Life teaches that your true essence is spiritual, infinite, and eternal!

In closing out this first chapter, affirm with me: "God is Love, I am Love... I am One with Source above!"

Coming Up Next...
Learn in the next chapter how we can reconnect our mind and spirit to Divine creative consciousness through practicing the laws of Mind and Mental Mastery!

CHAPTER TWO:
The 7 Laws of Mind and Mental Mastery

Thoughts are causal energy and governed by invisible law...

In a world driven by rapid change, external pressures, and constant noise, the power of the human mind remains one of the most underutilized forces for transformation. At the heart of personal success, emotional well-being, and spiritual growth lies a profound truth: our thoughts shape our reality. The Laws of Mind—universal principles governing thought, belief, and consciousness—offer a timeless framework for harnessing this inner power. Mental mastery is not about control in the traditional sense, but about alignment with these laws to cultivate clarity, purpose, and resilience.

Understanding the Laws of Mind equips us with the ability to direct our thoughts constructively, reprogram limiting beliefs, and create harmony between our inner world and outer experiences. Living by these laws requires discipline, self-awareness, and intentionality—but the rewards are immeasurable. From increased confidence and creativity to healing, peace of mind, and a sense of divine connection, mental mastery unlocks the potential that lies dormant in every human being.

This journey is not merely theoretical; it is deeply practical. By understanding and applying these laws in daily life, we begin to experience tangible shifts—doors open, relationships improve, and obstacles dissolve. The mind, when governed wisely, becomes not a battleground but a sacred space for creation. In embracing the principles of mental mastery, we awaken to our true power and begin to shape our lives with purpose and grace.

Human life is not shaped solely by external events, but far more powerfully by internal realities—by the thoughts we think, the beliefs we hold, and the expectations we nurture. These inner forces operate according to precise and immutable principles known as the Laws of Mind. To live a fulfilled, empowered, and purpose-driven life, it is essential to not only understand these laws but to live in conscious alignment with them. Mental mastery is the art and practice of doing just that: mastering our inner world to transform our outer experience!

To know and live by the following seven laws of mind is to move from unconscious reaction to conscious proactive creation. It is to reclaim the power of your mind as the architect of your destiny. Mental mastery is not about force, but alignment. It is not about striving, but allowing the natural laws of mind to work in your favor.

When you live in harmony with these laws, life begins to unfold with greater ease, joy, and purpose—and you step fully into the role of conscious co-creator of your reality!

Law of Mind and Mental Mastery #1:
The Law of Cause and Effect

Principle:
Thoughts are causes and conditions are effect.

"Whatever a man sows (*mentally*) that shall he also reap (*attract*).
– Galatians 6:7

The first step of good Mental Health and Mastery is to understand the **Law of Cause and Effect**, which teaches us that every thought is a cause and every condition a corresponding effect. Nothing in our lives happens by chance; it is all the result of mental activity. To change the conditions of our lives, we must first change the causes—our dominant thoughts, attitudes, and beliefs.

The biblical principle "Whatever a man sows, that shall he also reap" (Galatians 6:7) perfectly reflects the Law of Cause and Effect. Spiritually and mentally, every thought, belief, and intention we plant in the mind acts as a seed. These seeds grow into the experiences, circumstances, and conditions we later encounter in life.

When we sow thoughts of love, faith, abundance, and integrity, we reap blessings, peace, and progress. But when we sow thoughts of fear, bitterness, or lack, we attract struggle, confusion, or delay. This law reminds us that our inner life creates our outer world.

Key insight: To reap a harvest of good, we must be intentional about what we plant mentally. Guard your thoughts, nurture what is life-giving, and trust that the results will reflect the seeds you've sown.

On the quantum level, the Law of Cause and Effect reveals itself not as rigid, mechanical reaction, but as a dance of **interconnected influence**. Every thought, intention, and action sends out energy into the quantum field—ripples that interact with the web of reality, shaping what returns to us.

In classical physics, cause and effect are linear: A leads to B. But in quantum physics, the relationship is more subtle and multidimensional. **The observer affects the outcome** simply by focusing attention. **Entangled particles influence each other instantly**, regardless of distance—suggesting that cause and effect can be non-local, beyond space and time.

This means that **our inner world—our beliefs, emotions, and intentions—can be causal forces**, shaping not only our experiences but the reality we draw toward us.

So, **on the quantum level, the Law of Cause and Effect is not just about external actions—it's about the frequency we emit. What we send out into the field, consciously or unconsciously, returns to us in resonance.** Reality reflects the energetic causes we set in motion.

Application:

Applying the Law of Cause and Effect for a more Transcendent Life...

> The Law of Cause and Effect teaches that every thought, word, and action is a cause that sets into motion a corresponding effect. Nothing happens by accident—your current circumstances are the result of past causes, and your future will be shaped by what you choose now. To live intentionally, you must become the conscious cause of the outcomes you desire.

To apply this law:

- Take full responsibility for your thoughts, choices, and actions.
- Recognize that if you want different results, you must create different causes.
- Align your daily mindset and behaviors with the outcomes you seek—be the cause of peace, success, love, or abundance.

Mindfulness Practice:

Use the *"Cause-to-Effect Reflection."*

1. At the end of each day, take 5–10 minutes to reflect on one area of your life you want to improve. Ask: *What causes am I setting into motion here? Are my thoughts, beliefs, and actions aligned with the outcome I desire?*

2. Write your insights in a journal and set one small intention the next day to shift a cause toward a better effect.

Final Thought:

*The **Law of Cause and Effect** teaches that life is not random—it **is responsive**. Our thoughts are not empty; they are **creative forces**, shaping our world moment by moment. As we think, so we become. When we align our thoughts with the highest good—for ourselves and for others—we create not only better conditions, but a better world.*

Law of Mind and Mental Mastery #2: **The Law of Control**

Principle:
The only thing you can really control is your thoughts.

The **Law of Thought Control** reminds us that we have the ability—and the responsibility—to govern what we allow to occupy our minds. Just as we would guard a garden from weeds, we must guard our minds from fear, doubt, and negativity. Mental mastery begins with disciplining the mind to focus only on what serves growth, truth, and well-being.

The Apostle Paul in 2 Corinthians 10:5 speaks of this saying we should be "bringing every thought into captivity" as **the Law of Control teaches that we are the ultimate authority over our thoughts—and where our mind consistently goes, our energy naturally follows.** When we direct our attention toward fear, doubt, or negativity, we feed and strengthen those conditions. But when we choose to focus on peace, purpose, and possibility, we channel our energy into creating empowering outcomes. *"Where my mind goes, energy flows"* is a powerful reminder that by consciously guiding our thoughts, we direct the creative force of our lives. Control your mind, and you control your energy—control your energy, and you shape your destiny.

On the quantum level, the universe is a field of infinite possibilities, where outcomes are not fixed until they are observed. This means reality responds to **consciousness**—and the only thing we truly have control over is our **own thoughts.** The Law of Control teaches that while we cannot control people, events, or the external world, we can **choose our focus, beliefs, and responses.** In quantum terms, this is powerful: the **observer**

effect shows that what we pay attention to shapes what becomes real. Our thoughts collapse possibilities into outcomes.
When we take control of our thinking—directing it toward love, clarity, and truth—we align with the quantum field in a creative, empowered way. We stop reacting to chaos and start co-creating with intention.

Thus, on the quantum level, the Law of Control reminds us that true power is inner power. By mastering our thoughts, we influence the field—and shape the reality that reflects back to us.

Application:

Applying the Law of Thought Control for a more Transcendent Life...

The Law of Thought Control teaches that you have the power to choose and direct your thoughts, rather than allowing them to run unchecked. By consciously monitoring your inner dialogue and shifting negative or limiting thoughts to empowering ones, you begin to reshape your mental environment—and by extension, your reality.

To apply this law:

- Become aware of your habitual thoughts throughout the day.
- Notice when you're thinking in ways that promote fear, doubt, or limitation.
- Gently interrupt those patterns and replace them with thoughts that reflect your goals, values, and truth.

Mindfulness Practice:

Try the *"Mental Substitution Exercise."*

1. For one week, every time you catch yourself thinking something negative (e.g., "I can't do this"), immediately replace it with a positive, present-tense affirmation (e.g., "I am capable and growing stronger every day").

2. Write down repeated negative thoughts and their positive replacements in a journal. This practice helps rewire your mind and strengthens your ability to take control of your inner world.

Consistent practice leads to greater clarity, emotional balance, and the ability to create from a place of intention rather than reaction.

Final Thought:

Freedom doesn't come from controlling the world—it comes from mastering your mind! **The Law of Control reminds us that when we control our thoughts,** *we control our* **direction,** *our* **emotions,** *and our* **destiny.** *In that mastery lies the doorway to peace, power, and the Transcendent life we were created to live!*

Law of Mind and Mental Mastery #3:
The Law of Belief

Principle:
Whatever You Believe with Feeling Becomes Your Reality

The Law of Belief declares: *what you believe with feeling becomes your reality*. Beliefs are not idle ideas—they are active creative forces that shape perception, behavior, and outcomes. Whether empowering or limiting, your beliefs condition your experience. Therefore, changing your beliefs changes your life! Proverbs 23:7 states, *"As a man thinketh, so is he!"*

The Law of Belief states that what you deeply believe— especially when it is charged with strong emotion—shapes your experience of life. Your subconscious mind accepts your beliefs as truth and works to make them real, whether they empower or limit you. When you believe something with feeling, you impress it upon your inner mind, which then influences your actions, perceptions, and even the opportunities you attract.

If you believe you are worthy, capable, and supported, your reality will reflect those truths. But if you believe you're not enough or that success is out of reach, you'll unconsciously create circumstances to confirm that.

Key insight:
To change your reality, first change your beliefs—and charge them with faith, emotion, and repetition. Belief, combined with feeling, becomes a powerful creative force.

On the quantum level, reality is not solid and fixed—it is a field of infinite potential, shaped by consciousness. The Law of Belief teaches that **your deeply held beliefs—especially those charged with emotion—act as instructions to the quantum field**, determining which possibilities become real for you.

In quantum physics, the **observer effect** shows that the act of observation influences what manifests. But it's not just passive observation—it's belief, intention, and emotional energy that carry the most influence. When you believe something with strong feeling, you send out a coherent, focused vibration that interacts with the quantum field, collapsing potential into form.

Whether your belief is empowering or limiting, the quantum field doesn't judge—it simply mirrors back the frequency you consistently hold.

So, on the quantum level, the Law of Belief means this: what you emotionally accept as true becomes your lived experience. Change your belief, and you shift your reality.

Application:

Applying the Law of Belief for a Transcendent Life...

The Law of Belief teaches that your deeply held beliefs—especially those felt with emotion—shape your reality. What you believe about yourself, others, and life becomes the filter through which you experience everything. To transform your life, you must identify and consciously reshape limiting beliefs into empowering ones.

To apply this law:

- Begin by observing recurring patterns in your life. Ask: *What belief might be creating this experience?*

- Challenge beliefs that hold you back, such as "I'm not good enough" or "Success is for other people."
- Replace them with new, empowering beliefs that align with the life you want to live.

Mindfulness Practice:

Try the *"Belief Rewriting Method."*

1. Identify one limiting belief you hold (e.g., "I always fail at new things").
2. Write down a new belief to replace it (e.g., "I learn and grow stronger with every new experience").
3. For 7 days, repeat the new belief out loud with strong emotion every morning and evening. Visualize yourself already living from that truth.

With consistency and emotional conviction, your new belief will begin to take root—reshaping not only how you think, but how you live.

Final Thought:

The Law of Belief teaches that the world within precedes the world without. When we believe with feeling, we participate in the Divine act of creation itself. By aligning our beliefs with love, abundance, and purpose, we invite a reality that reflects the highest expression of who we truly are.

Law of Mind and Mental Mastery #4:
The Law of Expectation

Principle:
You get what you expect... Always expect the best!

The **Law of Expectation** states that *you get what you expect*. Expectation is a form of mental magnetism. When you confidently expect good, good tends to follow. When you expect failure or disappointment, you unknowingly pave the way for their arrival. Your expectations act like a blueprint for your future.

The scripture *"Eye has not seen, nor ear heard, neither has entered into the heart of man, the things which God has prepared for those who love Him"* (1 Corinthians 2:9) beautifully aligns with the **Law of Expectation**. This law teaches that what you confidently expect tends to become your reality—yet even our highest expectations can fall short of the limitless good God has prepared for us.

This verse reminds us that divine potential far exceeds human imagination. When we align our expectations with faith, love, and trust in divine goodness, we open ourselves to receive blessings beyond anything we've hoped for or imagined. Expectation, then, becomes an act of spiritual readiness—preparing our hearts and minds to receive what God has already prepared.

Key insight:
Raise your expectations, not just based on what you can see, but on what God promises. Expect divine abundance, healing, and guidance—even when it hasn't yet appeared—knowing that something greater is always being prepared for you.

At the quantum level, the universe responds to the observer's consciousness. The Law of Expectation states that what we consistently expect, especially with emotional conviction, becomes a self-fulfilling prophecy—because we are projecting those expectations into the quantum field.

In quantum physics, **the observer doesn't just witness reality— they influence it**. Expectation acts like a filter, focusing attention and energy on certain outcomes, and unconsciously guiding decisions, emotions, and behaviors to match. The field reflects back what we consistently anticipate—not just what we hope for, but what we *truly* expect.

When we expect the worst, we collapse possibilities toward that negative outcome. But when we expect the best—with faith, gratitude, and confidence—we align with higher, more positive potentials and bring them into fruition.

So, on the quantum level, the Law of Expectation reminds us: Expectation is projection... so project the best, and the field will organize to reflect it!

Application:

Applying the Law of Expectation for a Transcendent Life...

> The Law of Expectation teaches that what you consistently and confidently expect—good or bad—tends to manifest in your life. Your expectations shape your attitude, energy, and actions, influencing how people and situations respond to you. When you expect the best, you naturally align your mind, emotions, and behavior with positive outcomes.

To apply this law:

- Pay attention to your dominant expectations in key areas of life (health, relationships, finances, etc.).
- Replace negative expectations with confident, faith-filled ones that reflect what you truly desire.
- Speak and act as if your desired outcome is already on its way.

Mindfulness Practice:

Use the *"Positive Expectation Reset."*

1. Each morning, choose one area of your life and declare out loud: *"I expect the best in [this area]. I am open and ready for good things to unfold."*

2. Hold that expectation throughout the day, especially when doubts arise. Reinforce it by visualizing your desired outcome as already real.

Over time, this practice conditions your mind to expect good— and your life will begin to rise to meet that expectation.

Final Thought:

By mastering the Law of Expectation, we step into the role of conscious creators of our reality. When we always expect the best, we not only attract blessings but also strengthen our resilience and joy. Expect greatness, and watch your life unfold accordingly!

Law of Mind and Mental Mastery #5: The Law of Attraction

Principle:

*"The law of Attraction is working all the time
and is manifesting seen and unseen thoughts and emotions
no matter whether positive or negative
our greatest hopes and fears become realized
according to the conscious and unconscious thought energy
in one's heart and mind!"* – Isaac Heckman

The **Law of Attraction** is the principle that like attracts like. Your mental vibration—made up of your thoughts, feelings, and beliefs—connected to the quantum interwoven consciousness of all things – draws experiences that mirror your inner state. Positive thoughts attract positive outcomes; fear and worry attract their own reflection. To attract what you desire, you must become a vibrational match to it. Thus it is the magnetic power of the universe that draws similar energies together! It manifests through the power of creation. So in order to connect our minds with the mind of the creator we must visualize the world and life we desire with detailed and intense emotion keeping in our mind that picture and working towards it... especially visualizing just before sleep when the subconscious mind is the most receptive.

The Law of Attraction and the Principle of Thought, Feeling, AND Action

The **Law of Attraction** teaches that you invariably draw into your life what you consistently think about, feel deeply, and act upon. Most fail to see the law of attraction working because they are not working with belief and a clear detailed vision as if it already is. So remember, thought, feeling, and your action form a powerful triad of creation—working together to shape your experiences and outcomes.

- **Thought** sets the direction by focusing your mind on what you desire or fear.
- **Feeling** energizes the thought, giving it emotional charge and magnetism.
- **Action** grounds the thought into reality, signaling your belief and commitment to its manifestation.

   When your thoughts are clear, your feelings are aligned with belief and joy, and your actions support your vision, you become a magnetic force for your desired outcomes. But if your thoughts, emotions, and actions are in conflict, you send mixed signals—and the results reflect that confusion.

To consciously use the Law of Attraction, think clearly about what you want with detailed clarity, feel it as if it's already real, and take inspired action toward it *keeping it in your mind and working toward it everyday.*. This alignment activates the creative power within and around you, drawing your vision into reality.

On the quantum level, everything is energy—including your thoughts, emotions, and beliefs. The Law of Attraction states that **like attracts like**: the frequency you consistently emit draws in matching experiences from the quantum field of infinite possibilities.

This law is **always active**, whether you're aware of it or not. Your conscious thoughts shape reality, but so do your unconscious beliefs, emotional patterns, and deep-seated expectations. The quantum field responds not just to what you *say* you want, but to what you consistently *feel and believe*—whether positive or negative.

Because thought and emotion are energy, they act as **magnetic signals**, attracting circumstances that resonate with them. That's why both your greatest hopes and your deepest fears can manifest—**whatever dominates your inner world becomes the blueprint for your outer world.**

So, on the quantum level, the Law of Attraction shows that your life is a reflection of the vibration you carry in your heart and mind—seen or unseen. To attract what you desire, you must first become it within.

Application:

Applying the Law of Attraction with Visualization Before Sleep

One of the most powerful times to apply the **Law of Attraction** is just before sleep, when your mind is in a relaxed, receptive state. In this state—between wakefulness and sleep—your subconscious is more open to suggestion, making it the perfect time to plant the seeds of your desires through visualization.
  To apply this law for a Transcendent Life...

- Each night before bed, focus your mind on a specific goal or desired outcome.
- Visualize it in vivid detail as if it's already happening—see it, feel it, and experience the joy and fulfillment of having it now.
- Let the emotions of success, gratitude, or peace fill your heart as you drift off to sleep.

Mindfulness Practice:

Use the *"Nighttime Visualization Ritual."*

1. Lie down and take a few deep breaths to relax your body and quiet your mind.
2. Close your eyes and imagine your ideal outcome—whether it's a goal achieved, a relationship healed, or a new opportunity unfolding.
3. Feel the emotions of already having it. Smile. Breathe it in.
4. End with a quiet affirmation: *"It is done. I receive it with gratitude."*

By consistently visualizing in this state, you impress your desires onto the subconscious, activating the Law of Attraction and drawing aligned opportunities and inspiration into your waking life.

Final Thought:

Manifestation is a sacred synergy. Thought inspires, feeling fuels, and action actualizes. Embrace all three and watch as your dreams unfold—not by chance, but by the deliberate power of your aligned being in accordance with the Law of Attraction!

Law of Mind and Mental Mastery #6: The Law of Correspondence

Principle:
Your outer world corresponds to your inner world.

The **Law of Correspondence** reveals that *as within, so without*. Your outer world is a direct reflection of your inner world. If there is chaos outside, it is a signal to bring harmony within. If peace, clarity, and purpose reign in your mind, they will also manifest in your surroundings.

The **Law of Correspondence** states that your external reality is a mirror of your internal state. The conditions, relationships, and experiences you encounter in the outer world correspond directly to the thoughts, beliefs, emotions, and attitudes you hold within.

If there is chaos, conflict, or lack in your environment, it often reflects inner confusion, fear, or limiting beliefs. Likewise, when your inner world is grounded in peace, clarity, confidence, and love, your outer life begins to reflect those qualities through harmony, opportunity, and fulfillment.

On the quantum level, this is more than philosophy—it's proven by physics! Quantum theory shows that **the observer affects the observed.** Your thoughts, beliefs, and emotions are energy, and they interact with the quantum field—the invisible realm of potential that shapes all matter and experience. What you hold within—whether consciously or subconsciously—sends vibrational signals that collapse possibilities into actual outcomes.

This means that your outer circumstances **correspond to the frequency of your inner world.** Fear and conflict within attract confusion and struggle without. Peace, love, and clarity within draw harmony and opportunity without.

So, on the quantum level, the Law of Correspondence confirms that the world you experience is not separate from you—it's a mirror of your inner vibration. Change your inner world, and your outer world shifts in response.

Key insight:
To change your outer circumstances, you must first transform your inner world. Heal the root within, and the branches of your life will flourish. When you align your mind and heart with truth and purpose, your reality begins to correspond in powerful and positive ways.

Application:

Applying the Law of Correspondence for a Transcendent Life...

The **Law of Correspondence** teaches that your outer world is a reflection of your inner world. To change what you see around you—whether in relationships, finances, health, or success—you must first examine and align what's happening within your mind and heart.

To apply this law:

- Pay attention to patterns in your life that feel out of balance.

- Ask yourself: *What thoughts, beliefs, or emotions within me might be creating or attracting this experience?*

- Make inner shifts by changing your mindset, healing emotional blocks, and aligning with higher truth.

Mindfulness Practice:

Try the *"Mirror Check-In."*

1. Once a day, reflect on a challenge or situation in your outer world. Write down what it might be mirroring from within—such as fear, self-doubt, or lack of self-worth.

2. Then write a new, empowering thought to shift your inner state (e.g., *"I am worthy of harmony and support"*). Affirm and meditate on this new belief daily.

Final Thought:

As you align your inner world with clarity, peace, and purpose, your outer world will begin to reflect the same.

Law of Mind and Mental Mastery #7:
The Law of Superconscious Activity

Principle:
Any thought, plan, goal or idea (whether positive or negative) if held continuously in your conscious mind must be brought into reality by your super-conscious mind.

The **Law of Superconscious Activity** invites us to access the highest part of our being—the superconscious mind. This is the realm of intuition, inspiration, divine guidance, and limitless creativity. When we quiet the noise of the lower mind and align with this higher intelligence, we unlock extraordinary potential and insight.

The **Law of Superconscious Activity** states that any thought, plan, goal, or idea—whether positive or negative—that is held continuously in your conscious mind will eventually be accepted and acted upon by your **superconscious mind**, bringing it into your reality. The superconscious is the higher part of your mind connected to divine intelligence, creativity, and limitless potential. It works beyond logic, time, and effort to orchestrate people, circumstances, and ideas that align with your dominant focus.

Whether you are aware of it or not, the superconscious is always responding to your mental patterns. The clearer and more emotionally charged your focus, the more powerfully it works to fulfill it.

On the quantum level, reality unfolds through the interplay of different layers of consciousness. The **conscious mind** generates thoughts, plans, goals, and ideas—sending focused energy into the quantum field. However, the actual **manifestation** requires activation by the **superconscious mind**, the deeper, higher-level aspect of awareness that connects directly with the infinite quantum field of possibilities.

When you hold a thought or goal continuously in your conscious mind—whether positive or negative—it acts like a signal sent into the quantum field. The superconscious mind then organizes the subtle energies and coordinates the invisible forces needed to bring that intention into form.

This means that nothing merely imagined or planned stays unrealized if it remains truly sustained in conscious focus. The **superconscious acts as the creative engine, translating your persistent mental energy into physical reality** by guiding the quantum potentials to collapse into the experience aligned with your focus.

Thus, on the quantum level, the Law of Superconscious Activity shows how sustained conscious intention activates deeper creative forces to manifest your inner visions in the outer world.

Key to remember: Keep your thoughts aligned with your highest intentions. Focus consistently on what you truly desire—not on what you fear. Trust that your superconscious mind is always working behind the scenes to make your inner vision your outer reality.

Application:

Applying the Law of Superconscious Activity for a Transcendent Life...

The **Law of Superconscious Activity** teaches that your superconscious mind—your highest, most creative inner power connected to Divine Mind—automatically works to bring into reality any thought, goal, or vision you hold with clarity and emotion. When you focus consistently on a desire with faith and purpose, your superconscious goes to work behind the scenes, aligning people, opportunities, and ideas to fulfill it.

To apply this law:

- Choose a clear, meaningful goal or desire and impress it deeply into your conscious mind through daily focus.
- Visualize it as already accomplished, feel the joy of it, and affirm its reality with confidence.
- Let go of "how" it will happen—trust your superconscious mind to guide and orchestrate the path and simply have an attitude of calm, confident positive expectations.

Mindfulness Practice:

Try the *"Superconscious Programming Ritual."*

1. Each morning and evening, spend 3-5 minutes visualizing your goal as if it is already complete. Say aloud:

   "This or something better is now being fulfilled through divine intelligence. I trust my superconscious mind to lead the way."

2. Stay consistent. As you hold the vision and take inspired action, your superconscious will do the invisible work to bring it into your life—often in ways more perfect than you imagined.

Final Thought:

The Law of Superconscious Activity reminds us that we are not alone on our journey. Divine wisdom is always present, ready to inspire, heal, and elevate. When we open ourselves to this sacred source, we become co-creators in the grand unfolding of life, guided by a power far greater than our own.

Chapter Summary/Key Takeaways

In summary, Higher Mind Consciousness is Causal Energy that affects everything in Life! Lower limited thoughts, limit you... but Divinely powerful thoughts empower you... For if your mind can conceive it, you can achieve it!

Remember the 7 Laws of Higher Mind and Mastery:
1) **Thoughts are causes** and conditions are effect.
2) The only thing you can really **control** is **your thoughts**.
3) Whatever you **believe** with feeling, becomes your reality.
4) You get what you expect, so **expect the best**!
5) Think about what you want with intense emotion and clarity and keep it in your mind and work toward it everyday in order to set **the Law of Attraction** in motion.
6) Your **outer world corresponds to your inner world and visa versa**.
7) Any thought if held continuously in your conscious mind must be brought into reality by your **super-conscious mind**.

Coming Up Next...
As powerful as the mind is, it is even more powerful when combined with the feelings of the heart! In the next chapter you will learn about the seven Laws of Emotional "Heart" Health!

CHAPTER THREE:
The 7 Laws of Emotion and "Heart" Health

The Importance of Knowing and Living by the Laws of Emotion is that it helps us understand that emotions are not random reactions—they are the result of deeply rooted internal laws that shape how we interpret and respond to life. Just as the mind operates according to certain principles, so too does our emotional life. Understanding and living in alignment with the 7 Laws of Emotion is essential for cultivating emotional intelligence, inner peace, and long-term mental and spiritual well-being.

These 7 laws govern how we experience joy, sadness, fear, anger, love, and guilt. They help us understand *why* we feel what we feel—and more importantly, how we can respond with wisdom rather than be controlled by unconscious emotional patterns. In short, we will look into understanding and applying the following 7 laws that govern our Emotional Heath:

The Law of Identity teaches that we feel emotions based on who we believe we are. When our identity is rooted in truth and spiritual wholeness, we experience emotional stability.

The Law of Situational Meaning reveals that it's not events themselves, but the meaning we assign to them, that determines our emotional response. By changing our interpretation, we can shift how we feel.

The Law of Desire and Attachment shows how emotional suffering often arises when we cling too tightly to specific outcomes or unmet desires. Releasing attachment opens the way to peace.

The Law of Concern highlights that we are emotionally affected only by what we care about. Understanding our concerns helps us focus our energy wisely.

The Law of Apparent Reality explains that we emotionally respond to what seems real to us in the moment—even if it's not objectively true. Training the mind to see clearly can transform our emotions.

The Law of Comparative Feeling reminds us that emotions often arise from comparisons—between ourselves and others, or between what we have and what we think we should have. Gratitude and presence help dissolve unnecessary emotional conflict.

The Law of Judgment and Guilt shows how self-condemnation and harsh inner judgment create emotional pain. Healing comes through forgiveness, compassion, and truthful self-evaluation.

By learning and living in harmony with these emotional laws, we gain the power to navigate life with greater resilience, clarity, and compassion. We stop being victims of our emotions and become stewards of them—using each feeling as a signal, a teacher, and a gateway to deeper self-awareness and spiritual growth.

Law of Emotional Health #1:
The Law of Identity

Principle:
How we view ourselves in our core identity will shape how we feel about ourselves, how we manifest and what energy we attract.

The **Law of Identity** states that **who you believe you are** determines how you think, feel, act, and ultimately live. Your self-concept—your inner "I AM"—forms the root of your reality. When you identify with fear, lack, or limitation, your life reflects those patterns. But when you identify with truth, love, purpose, and divine worth, you begin to manifest a life aligned with those qualities.

This law reminds us that **transformation begins not with effort, but with identity**. The more you align with your true spiritual self, the more your life becomes an authentic expression of inner truth.

On the quantum level, it is revealed that your **emotions are not fixed**—they an energetic pattern formed by your beliefs, self-concept, and inner narrative. The Law of Identity teaches that **your outer life is a direct reflection of your inner identity**—what you truly believe yourself to be, deep in your subconscious. The quantum field responds to frequency, not just desire. Your self-concept emits a constant vibration, and that vibration **attracts matching circumstances, relationships, and outcomes**.

If you see yourself as limited or unworthy, the field reflects lack and struggle. But when you align your identity with your true Divine nature—whole, worthy, and empowered—you shift your frequency to match abundance, peace, and purpose.

As you consistently affirm and embody your true, divine identity, your reality reshapes around it. This brings a deep **calm, humble confidence**, rooted not in ego, but in truth. And from that place, your emotional health stabilizes, because you're no longer chasing identity—you're living from it.

So on the quantum level, the Law of Identity reveals this: your life mirrors who you believe you are. Align with your divine self, and your world will begin to mirror your wholeness.

Key Insight: *Your outer life is shaped by your inner identity. Align your self-concept with your Divine nature, and your world will begin to reflect your true self!*

Application:

To apply this law, for more Transcendent Living, you must consciously **choose and affirm your true spiritual identity**—not based on past experiences or labels, but on your inner divine nature. It means shifting from saying "I am not enough" to "I am whole, worthy, and empowered by Divine Life."

How to Apply the Law of Identity

1. **Become Aware of Your Self-Talk**
   - Notice how often you say "I am" followed by something disempowering (e.g., "I'm not good enough," "I'm always anxious").
   - Recognize that these statements are not facts—they're identity scripts that can be rewritten.

2. **Affirm Your True Nature**

- Begin affirming who you truly are: a creation of love, light, and purpose.
- Replace limiting labels with empowering truths.

3. **Act in Harmony with Your Chosen Identity**
   - Let your new identity guide your actions. Ask: *"How does someone who believes this about themselves show up in the world?"*

Mindfulness Practice:

"Practice "Re-aligning to your Higher Identity"

1. Each morning, stand before a mirror, look into your eyes, and speak aloud 3–5 positive identity statements that begin with "I AM."
   - Example: "I AM a child of Light. I am loved. I am powerful in peace."
   - Example: "I am guided by Divine Wisdom."
2. Throughout the day, if you catch yourself identifying with fear or failure, **pause** and replace it with a conscious "I AM" truth.

Final Thought:

Your identity is not fixed by the past—it is formed by what you choose to believe today. As you consciously align with your higher identity, your life begins to rise to meet it.

Law of Emotional Health #2:
The Law of Situational Meaning

Principle:
We should not be situational with our love but unconditional.

The Law of Situational Meaning teaches that your emotional experience is not caused by events themselves, but by the meaning you assign to those events. Two people can experience the same situation and feel entirely different emotions—because their interpretation, not the event, creates their emotional reality.

This law reveals your power: you may not control what happens, but you can always choose how to see it. When you reframe situations through the lens of growth, faith, and purpose, your emotional state and outcomes shift accordingly.

On the quantum level, reality is shaped by the observer. This includes not just what we see, but how we **interpret** what we experience. The Law of Situational Meaning teaches that **our emotional reality is not determined by events themselves, but by the meaning we assign to them.**

In quantum physics, the same wave of potential can become different outcomes depending on how it is observed. Likewise, two people can experience the same event but feel completely different emotions—because their **beliefs, perceptions, and inner narratives** shape the meaning they assign to it.

Meaning is fluid; it can shift as our beliefs evolve. But **real, selfless love**—the highest vibrational frequency—is constant and unchanging. It transcends situations and sees through to the eternal truth beyond temporary appearances.

The more we align with this **unconditional love**, the more our thoughts and emotions become **stable, clear, and elevated**. Instead of being tossed by changing meanings and reactions, we live from a higher perspective—rooted in love, not fear.

So, on the quantum level, the Law of Situational Meaning reveals: your inner world shapes your emotional reality through meaning—but unconditional love aligns you with the unchanging truth, bringing peace and emotional consistency beyond circumstance.

Application:

How to Apply the Law of Situational Meaning for more Transcendent Living...

By consciously choosing more empowering, compassionate, or faith-filled meanings, we rise above victimhood and step into transcendent living—where growth, peace, and divine purpose guide our perception.

Instead of asking, *"Why is this happening to me?"* ask, *"What is this teaching me?"* or *"How can I grow through this?"* This mindset transforms pain into wisdom and setbacks into stepping stones. It allows us to live with deeper trust, clarity, and resilience—rooted in spiritual awareness rather than reaction.

- Catch and Question Your Interpretation

    When you feel triggered, ask: *"What am I making this mean?"* Separate the **event** from your **story** about the event.

- Choose an Empowering Meaning

    Reframe challenges as opportunities for growth, realignment, or trust.

Turn "This is happening to me" into "This is happening **for** me."

Practice Gratitude for Lessons in Disguise

Recognize that meaning can evolve—what seems negative now may reveal hidden purpose later.

Mindfulness Practice:

"Meaning Shift Reflection"

Each evening, write down one challenging or emotional moment from your day.

Reflect:

1. What did I originally make it mean?
2. What else could it mean from a higher perspective?
3. What growth or wisdom can I take from it?

Final Thought:

The Law of Situational Meaning reveals that everything we perceive is usually interpreted according to the meaning we assign to it. Every event, challenge, or success in our life is filtered through the lens of our perspective. What seems like an obstacle to one person can become a doorway to growth for another. When we awaken to this law, we reclaim the power to define our reality. We are not victims of circumstance but interpreters of it, capable of transforming pain into purpose and setbacks into sacred shifts. By choosing empowering meanings in every situation, we elevate our consciousness and step into the wisdom of a truly transcendent life!

Law of Emotional Health #3:
The Law of Desire and Attachment

Principle:
The less we identify with something and emotionally desire and/or attach ourselves to anything - the happier we will be.

The **Law of Desire and Attachment** teaches that while desire is a natural force of creation and movement, **attachment to the outcome creates suffering**. When you cling to a specific result, you create tension, fear, and resistance—blocking the very flow you are trying to align with.

Desire in itself is not the problem—it's the emotional dependence on having things *exactly* your way or in your timing that causes stress, disappointment, or even obsession. When you **detach from the outcome** and trust the higher order of life, you remain peaceful, open, and aligned with what's truly best for your growth and purpose.

On the quantum level, the universe operates through vibration, resonance, and flow—not force or clinging. The Law of Desire and Attachment teaches that **the more we cling to or over-identify with something—whether an outcome, object, or identity—the more we create resistance in the quantum field.**

Desire in itself is natural—it sets intention and focus. But **attachment**, which is the fear of not having or losing something, creates a low-frequency vibration of lack, fear, and control. This disrupts the coherent energy needed to manifest or attract, and it blocks the free flow of possibilities in the quantum field.

Paradoxically, when we let go of attachment and simply **trust**, we align with the natural intelligence of the universe. **Non-attachment raises our frequency,** allowing the quantum field to respond with ease and grace. Happiness and peace arise, not from getting what we crave, but from **freedom from craving**.

So on the quantum level, the Law of Desire and Attachment reveals: the less you cling, the more you flow—and the freer and happier you become. Non-attachment aligns you with the effortless unfolding of your highest good.

Application:

How to Apply the Law of Desire and Attachment for a more Transcendent Life...

Emotional suffering often arises not from what happens to us, but from clinging to how we think things should be. The practice of detachment doesn't mean giving up desire—it means releasing the need to *control* outcomes or *derive identity* from them. When we detach, we free ourselves from disappointment, anxiety, and fear, creating space for peace, trust, and inner liberation.
To live a more transcendent life, hold your desires lightly. Let go of needing people, possessions, or circumstances to validate your worth or determine your happiness. Trust that life, guided by divine wisdom, will bring what is truly meant for you.

Clarify Your Desire:

Identify what you truly want—but go deeper: *Why do you want it? What feeling are you really seeking (peace, love, purpose)?*

Release the Grasp:

Trust: *"This or something better will come in its own time. I trust the timing and wisdom of Life."*

Then let go of needing your original desire that defined your idea of worth or happiness. Gently affirm: *"I release this with love. I trust in a higher outcome."*

Focus on the Process, Not the Possession:

Pour your energy into inspired action and trust—not into control or anxiety.

Mindfulness Practice:

"Surrendering Desire and Attachment Meditation"

Each morning or evening:
1. Sit quietly and visualize your desire as already fulfilled.
2. Feel the joy, gratitude, and peace it brings.
3. Say:

    "I release this into Divine timing. I remain open, guided, and unattached."

Final Thought:

Desire is the spark of movement, but **detachment is the path to freedom.** *When you release control, you create space for greater outcomes, peace, and divine alignment to unfold.*

Law of Emotional Health #4:
The Law of Concern

Principle:
We feel because we care about something.

The **Law of Concern** teaches that **your emotional energy follows your attention**—and when you **over-concern yourself with what is outside your control**, you deplete your peace, focus, and power. While caring is natural and compassionate, **excessive concern leads to anxiety, frustration, and disempowerment.**

This law invites you to discern between **what is yours to carry and what is not**. True inner peace comes from aligning your care with your sphere of influence, and surrendering what lies beyond it to a higher order or divine wisdom.

On the quantum level, emotion is energy in motion, and what we care about carries emotional charge. The Law of Concern teaches that we feel strong emotions—joy, fear, sadness, love—**because we are connected to what we value.** This emotional energy signals what matters to us and shapes how we interact with the quantum field.

Caring is a high-frequency state—especially when rooted in **loving-kindness**, compassion, and empathy. But when concern becomes **clinging, fear, or control**, it lowers our vibration and creates interference in the natural flow of energy. This kind of attachment distorts the signal we send into the quantum field, often attracting confusion or resistance.

True concern honors the emotional connection without trying to control outcomes. It holds space for love without possession. This non-attached, compassionate energy keeps us aligned with

quantum coherence, where outcomes unfold with greater harmony and balance.

So on the quantum level, the Law of Concern shows us that healthy, heartfelt emotion empowers creation—when it flows from loving-kindness, not control. Care deeply, but let go lightly—and the universe responds with grace.

Application:

How to Apply the Law of Concern for more Transcendent Living...

When we focus only on what is within our power—our thoughts, responses, and prayers—we reclaim inner calm and become more effective helpers. We live wisely and peacefully, rather than anxiously and reactively.

> **Notice Where Your Energy Is Going:**
>
> > Ask: *"Am I worrying about something I cannot change?"*
> >
> > Bring your attention back to what you can influence: your thoughts, responses, and choices.
>
> **Shift from Worry to Wise Action:**
>
> > If a concern is within your power, take a step. If not, release it in trust or prayer.
> >
> > Replace worry with proactive support, boundaries, or faith.
>
> **Stay Rooted in Your Center:**
>
> > Let concern awaken compassion—not control or fear.

Mindfulness Practice:

"Circle of Control" Exercise

1. Draw two circles:
    - **Inner Circle:** What you can control (your mindset, actions, responses).
    - **Outer Circle:** What you cannot control (others' choices, outcomes, timing).
2. Focus your time and prayerful energy on the inner circle. Each time you feel anxious, bring your mind back to what is within your domain.

Final Thought:

You are not responsible for everything—only for how you respond. Let go of the burden of over-concern, and you will find clarity, peace, and the wisdom to act with purpose!

Law of Emotional Health #5:
The Law of Apparent Reality

Principle:
Whatever seems real to us, can elicit an emotional response. And what you feel emotionally to be true on the inside manifests as your reality on the outside!

The **Law of Apparent Reality** teaches that **what you emotionally feel to be true becomes your reality—even if it's not actually true.** Your mind accepts strong emotion as evidence, and your nervous system reacts accordingly. If you fear something deeply, it begins to feel real, even when it isn't. Over time, these perceptions shape your beliefs, decisions, and experiences.

This law reminds us to **distinguish between perception and truth**. Your emotional reactions are valid, but they don't always reflect reality. By becoming more aware of your inner narratives, you reclaim the power to choose how you respond—and what you allow to shape your world.

On the quantum level, reality is not fixed—it is a field of infinite possibilities, shaped by observation, intention, and most powerfully, **emotionally charged belief.** Quantum physics shows that the act of observation collapses potential into form. But it's not passive observation—it's the **emotional energy behind your thoughts** that gives them power. The subconscious mind doesn't distinguish between what's real and what's vividly imagined with feeling. So when you **feel something deeply— whether hopeful or fearful—the quantum field responds by aligning your outer circumstances to match that inner emotional "truth."**

This is why two people can live in the same world but experience very different realities—because each is projecting and receiving back from the field according to their inner emotional landscape.

So, on the quantum level, the Law of Apparent Reality reveals: your felt beliefs shape the form your life takes. Feel abundance, love, and possibility—and your reality begins to reflect it.

Application:

How to Apply the Law of Apparent Reality for more Transcendent Living...

1. **Pause and Observe**
   - When you feel overwhelmed, anxious, or reactive, ask:
   "Is this truly real, or just something I'm feeling very strongly right now?"

2. **Name the Emotion Without Judgment**
   - Saying, *"I feel afraid, but this doesn't mean I'm in danger,"* creates space between emotion and truth.

3. **Reframe the Narrative**
   - Replace emotional assumptions with grounded truths:
   "Just because I feel rejected doesn't mean I am unloved."

Mindfulness Practice:

"Reality Check Breath"

When you're caught in a strong emotional reaction:

1. Take 3 deep breaths.
2. Ask yourself:
   - "What am I assuming is true right now?"
   - "Is there evidence for it, or am I reacting to how it feels?"
3. Speak a calming truth to yourself, such as:

"Feelings are a physiological response to a way of thinking, but they are not always facts. I choose to see clearly."

Final Thought:

*Your emotions are powerful, but **they do not define what is true**. When you learn to pause, reflect, and question emotional assumptions, you move from illusion to clarity—and regain your spiritual and emotional freedom.*

Law of Emotional Health #6:
The Law of Comparative Feeling

Principle:
Looking at others can affect our expectations and feelings about ourselves.

The **Law of Comparative Feeling** teaches that we often don't evaluate our emotions in absolute terms—we evaluate them by **comparison**. Rather than asking, "Am I successful?" we ask, "Am I as successful as *that* person?" This tendency can distort our emotional experience, leading to envy, pride, discouragement, or false satisfaction based not on truth, but on how we *measure* ourselves against others.

When we compare, we often either inflate or diminish our self-worth. But the truth is, **you are on your own journey**, and true peace comes from **self-reference, not social comparison**.

On the quantum level, your energy—your thoughts, emotions, and self-perception—directly influences the reality you experience. The **Law of Comparative Feeling** teaches that when you compare yourself to others, especially from a place of lack or insecurity, you shift your vibration away from your authentic Divine alignment with the quantum field.

Comparison often triggers **low-frequency emotions** like envy, inadequacy, or pride. These distort your energetic signal, creating resistance in the field and attracting more experiences that mirror those feelings. The quantum field does not respond to truth or fairness—it responds to **what you emotionally feel and project**. When you feel "less than," you unknowingly create a reality that reflects that belief.

Looking at others through the lens of comparison pulls your focus outward and disconnects you from your own unique path and divine timing. But when you honor your own journey and tune into gratitude and self-worth, you send out a **coherent, empowered vibration** that the universe reflects back with clarity and support.

So, on the quantum level, the Law of Comparative Feeling reveals: comparison lowers your vibration and clouds your reality, but self-alignment to your true Higher Spiritual Self restores your power to shape a fulfilling and authentic life.

Application:

How to Apply the Law of Comparative Feeling for more Transcendent Living...

To live a more transcendent life, we must shift our inner lens. Instead of comparing, we choose gratitude. Instead of judging, we choose presence. By seeing our life as unique, purposeful, and divinely guided, we rise above the illusion of lack and embrace our own sacred path.

Catch Yourself Comparing

When you notice feelings like envy, inadequacy, or superiority, ask:
"Who am I comparing myself to right now—and why?"

Shift to Inner Alignment

Refocus on your personal values, goals, and growth.

Ask: *"Am I living in integrity with who I'm meant to be?"*

Celebrate Individuality

Recognize that others' success doesn't take away from your path—it can inspire without defining you.

Mindfulness Practice:

"Mirror vs. Window" Reflection

1. **Each evening**, write down one moment when you looked out a *"window"* (compared yourself to someone else).
2. Then reframe it into a *"mirror"*—What does this reveal about your own needs, values, or desires?
3. Example: "I felt envious of her confidence. Mirror: I desire to express myself more freely.
4. Practice: I will speak up in tomorrow's meeting."

Final Thought:

Comparison is a trap of the ego; growth is the path of the soul. True emotional freedom begins when you stop measuring your worth by others—and start honoring your unique unfolding.

Law of Emotional Health #7:
The Law of Judgement and Guilt

Principle:
Our emotions will be affected if we feel judged or condemned or if we feel guilt or shamed.

The **Law of Judgment and Guilt** teaches that whenever you judge yourself or others harshly, you create emotional conflict, separation, and inner heaviness. Judgment often leads to guilt, which is the emotional residue of feeling wrong, bad, or unworthy. While guilt can sometimes prompt positive change, **unresolved or excessive guilt becomes a burden**, distorting your sense of identity and blocking joy, peace, and connection with the Divine.

This law reveals a deeper truth: **compassion and conscious correction free us; judgment and guilt imprison us.** By replacing judgment with self-awareness and guilt with responsibility, we heal, grow, and return to alignment with grace.

As we discussed previously, **on the quantum level**, everything is interconnected—**a unified field of energy** where separation is an illusion. The Law of Judgment and Guilt teaches that whenever you **judge yourself or others harshly,** you create a vibrational distortion that disrupts your natural alignment with this field of Oneness.

Judgment and guilt are low-frequency emotions rooted in fear and separation. When you judge, you project division—creating an energetic signal that says, "I am separate from you," or "I am not enough." This emotional conflict sends incoherent vibrations into the quantum field, attracting more experiences of shame, rejection, or isolation.

Moreover, this judgment blinds you from the **truth of the Law of Oneness**—that we are all expressions of the same Source. When you condemn others, you condemn aspects of yourself. When you carry guilt, you block the flow of love, forgiveness, and healing that restores wholeness.

So, on the quantum level, the Law of Judgment and Guilt reveals: harsh judgment creates energetic separation, while compassion and forgiveness restore alignment with the unified field of love and Oneness.

Application:

How to Apply the Law of Judgment and Guilt for more Transcendent Living...

1. **Recognize Judgment as Projection**
   - When you judge others, pause and ask: *"What does this reflect in me?"*
   - When you judge yourself, ask: *"Am I punishing myself, or learning from this?"*

2. **Transform Guilt into Growth**
   - Instead of wallowing in guilt, reflect on what you can do differently.
   - Affirm: *"I am learning. I release the past and choose better."*

3. **Practice Self-Forgiveness**
   - Forgiveness is not denial—it's a conscious release of guilt through truth and love.

Mindfulness Practice:

"Release & Replace" Exercise

Each evening, reflect on any judgment or guilt from your day:

1. Write down what you judged or felt guilty about.
2. Ask:
   - *What did I learn from this?*
   - *What can I do better tomorrow?*
3. Say aloud or write:

"I forgive myself. I choose love over fear. I release guilt and return to truth."

Final Thought:

You are not your mistakes, and others are not theirs. **When you release judgment and guilt, you reclaim your power to heal, love, and grow—** *becoming more aligned with your highest self and divine purpose.*

Chapter Summary/Key Takeaways

In summary, your emotions are to be governed by your Higher Consciousness so as to align with and empower your positive mental manifestations... i.e. You are to rule your emotions, they are not to rule you, but are meant to serve you!

1) *Your identity is not fixed by the past—it is formed by what you choose to believe today*

2) *Your emotional experience is not caused by events themselves, but by the meaning you assign to those events*

3) *The less we identify with something or desire and/or attach ourselves – the happier we will be.*

4) *You are not responsible for everything—only for how you respond. Let go of the burden of over-concern, and you will find clarity, peace, and the wisdom to act with purpose!*

5) *What you feel emotionally to be true on the inside manifests as your reality on the outside*

6) *True emotional freedom begins when you stop measuring your worth by others—and start honoring your unique unfolding.*

7) *When you release judgment and guilt, you reclaim your power to heal, love, and grow*

Coming Up Next...
Our body is the physical vehicle of our spiritual soul, so it is very important to understand how to keep it in the best condition as how we treat our body affects our heart and mind as well! In the next chapter you will learn about the seven Laws of Physical Health!

CHAPTER FOUR:
The 7 Laws of Physical Health

Your body is not just flesh and bone—it is the **living, breathing temple** that houses your **spiritual soul**. Just as a vehicle carries a traveler on their journey, your body carries your soul through this earthly life. It is the medium through which you express divine purpose, fulfill your calling, and experience love, learning, and transformation.

Because of this sacred role, it is **vital to care for the body with reverence and intention**. A healthy, well-balanced body allows your spirit to shine more freely, your mind to think more clearly, and your heart to love more fully. When the body is neglected, overloaded, or disconnected from its divine purpose, your spiritual energy becomes dull, distracted, or even blocked.

Understanding how to maintain and honor your physical form—through nourishment, rest, movement, mindfulness, and alignment—empowers you to live a life of greater clarity, vitality, and spiritual fulfillment. Your body is not separate from your soul's mission—it is an essential part of it.

Health for the vessel of the earthly mother must be in harmony with the laws of the earth and that which comes from the earth naturally.

Law of Physical Health #1:
The Law of Nutrition

Principle:
"The earthly mother and I are "One" through my body"

Your bodily vessel comes from the minerals of the earth – and you need good living food grown from the earth for the body.

The **Law of Nutrition** teaches that the food you consume directly affects your physical health, emotional balance, mental clarity, and spiritual receptivity. **On the quantum level**, your body is not just physical matter—it is a **vibrating energy system**, constantly interacting with the energetic environment, including the food you eat. Similarly, food is not merely fuel—it is **vibrational energy**, and what you put into your body either supports or hinders your ability to live in harmony with your soul's purpose.

Just as the quality of fuel determines a vehicle's performance, the quality of your food determines your body's vitality and ability to serve your soul's mission, and the minerals and nutrients from the **Earth** carry a specific frequency that supports the optimal functioning of your physical vessel.

Whole, natural foods—rich in minerals, enzymes, and life-force—carry **coherent, bioavailable energy** that resonates with your body's own field. When you nourish your body with these earth-given substances, you support not just cellular health, but **energetic alignment**, vitality, and mental clarity.
In contrast, artificial, processed, or chemically altered foods can disrupt your body's energy field, creating dissonance and lowering your vibration. This affects not just physical health, but your **emotional and spiritual coherence** as well.

So, on the quantum level, the Law of Nutrition reveals: food is energy, and when you nourish your body with the pure elements of the earth, you align your vessel with higher frequencies—allowing your full potential to flow through a healthy, grounded, and vibrant form.

Advise: Dark green leafies are the best alkaline nutrient rich food as they absorb the nutrients from the earth below and life giving energy of the Creator's light from the sun above and store it and then transfer it to us when eaten, alkalizing our bodies and thus energizing and bringing life into our vessels. Next most important is fresh fruits and berries which are full of vitamins and anti-oxidants facilitating a long and healthy life! Avoid all carcinogenic foods and drinks as well as anything that makes your body acidic, as disease cannot grow in an alkaline body, but sickness and disease thrive in an acidic body.

Also it is important to remember to eat with awareness, gratitude, and intentionality, as you will nourish more than just the body—you will strengthen your connection between **body, mind, and spirit**. Living by this law means choosing foods that are life-giving, natural, and aligned with your body's true needs rather than reacting to emotional cravings or habits. Whole, living foods nourish your cells and raise your vibration, while processed, artificial, or excessive foods can dull your senses, disrupt inner harmony, and cloud spiritual awareness. To honor the law of nutrition is to **treat eating as a sacred act of self-respect and alignment.**

Application:

How to Apply the Law of Nutrition for Transcendent health and happiness...

- **Eat with Intention**

Choose foods that are living, whole, fresh, and energizing. Ask: *"Will this nourish me or deplete me?"*

- **Listen to Your Body's Wisdom**

    Pay attention to how foods make you feel—not just in the moment, but after eating.

- **Honor the Energy of Food**

    Bless your meals. Eat slowly. Acknowledge the source of your food as a gift of life and light.

Mindfulness Practice:

"Conscious Eating Ritual"

Once a day, practice a mindful meal:

1. Before eating, pause and take three deep breaths.
2. Say (or think):
3. "May this food nourish my body, uplift my mind, and support my spirit."
4. Eat slowly, without distraction. Focus on flavor, texture, and how your body responds.

Final Thought:

*Your body becomes what you consistently feed it—**not just physically, but energetically**. By choosing to nourish yourself with life-affirming foods, you honor your body as the sacred vessel of your soul and invite greater clarity, vitality, and spiritual alignment into your daily life.*

Law of Physical Health #2: The Law of Exercise

Principle:
Vitality and strength come through movement

Similar to the Spiritual **Law of Action in Chapter 1, The Law of Physical Movement, (i.e. Exercise)** teaches that **strength, vitality, and energy are developed through consistent movement.** Just as a muscle grows stronger when used, your body, mind, and spirit thrive when they are actively engaged. Without movement, stagnation sets in—physically through weakness, mentally through dullness, and spiritually through disconnection.

Exercise is not just a health habit; it is a **spiritual principle.** Movement awakens the body, clears the mind, and creates space for energy to flow. It reminds us that **life is dynamic**, and we are meant to move in harmony with its rhythms. Whether through walking, stretching, dancing, or structured workouts, **conscious movement restores vitality, clarity, and emotional well-being.**

On the quantum level, energy must move to stay coherent and vital. The **Law of Exercise** teaches that by physically moving your body, you activate the **Law of Action**—transforming potential energy into kinetic energy, and keeping your physical and energetic systems in harmonious flow.

Your body is a quantum instrument made of vibrating energy. Exercise stimulates circulation, oxygenation, and detoxification—not just physically, but energetically. Movement **amplifies your life force**, clears stagnation, and raises your vibration, making it easier for you to align with higher states of emotion, focus, and creativity.

When you act—through consistent, intentional movement—you signal to the quantum field that you are engaged with life, not passive. This creates momentum and draws in more **vitality, clarity, and synchronicity** in return.

So, on the quantum level, the Law of Exercise shows that moving your body energizes your field, activates the law of action, and aligns your physical vessel to support your highest expression of health and purpose.

Application:

How to Apply the Law of Exercise for Transcendent health and happiness...

Honor Movement as a Daily Ritual:

Treat exercise as a sacred appointment with yourself—not punishment, but empowerment.

Find what you enjoy: walking, yoga, cycling, strength training, or free movement.

Move with Presence:

As you exercise, connect with your breath and body. Feel the energy awaken in your limbs, spine, and heart.

Build Consistency Over Intensity

Daily, intentional movement—even in small amounts—leads to transformation over time.

Mindfulness Practice:

"Vitality Walk"

Each day, take a 10–20 minute walk outdoors (or in a peaceful space), and:

1. Breathe deeply with every step.
2. Repeat inwardly: "I move with purpose. I am strong. I am alive."
3. Let your thoughts clear and your energy renew as you move.
4. According to your ability, every day focus on giving each different muscle group in your body flexed (tightened) attention starting with your calves via raising up on your toes, then thighs through simple squats, then abs, then push-ups for chest, curls for arms, shrugs for traps and neck muscles and so on. This will keep your muscles from atrophy from a lack of use. Be active everyday as a sedentary life is the bodies' enemy.

Final Thought:

Movement is medicine. When you align your body with the natural law of exercise, you awaken the life force within you. **Strength is not just built in the muscles—it is built in the soul that chooses to move forward.**

Law of Physical Health #3:
The Law of Water

Principle:
Water enters with oxygen into the blood giving life as well as cleansing and circulation.

The **Law of Water** teaches that just as water is essential to all life on Earth, it is also fundamental to the life and flow within your body. Water represents **cleansing, flow, adaptability, and emotional balance.** Our bodies are composed of roughly 70% water—just like the Earth—revealing a sacred mirror between our inner landscape and the world around us... In both cases it is used for internally as well as externally for purification and cleansing, as well as the fact that it is a conduit of energy.

This law reminds us that **life thrives where water flows**—physically through hydration and cellular health, emotionally through released tears and inner healing, and spiritually through surrender and trust. When we align with the law of water, we become more fluid, peaceful, and clear—less rigid and reactive.

On the quantum level, water is not just a physical substance—it is a carrier of energy, memory, and vibration. The **Law of Water** teaches that proper hydration with pure, living water nourishes not only your physical cells but also supports the **flow of life force energy** throughout your entire being.

Furthermore, water molecules respond to intention, sound, and emotion—becoming **structured or chaotic** based on their energetic environment. When you drink clean, mineral-rich water, especially with gratitude or blessing, you are taking in a **high-frequency substance** that brings coherence to your body's energy field.

Water acts as a conductor for electrical signals in the body, aiding in cellular communication, detoxification, and the smooth flow of chi or prana. Dehydration creates energetic stagnation, weakening your field and your vitality.

So, on the quantum level, the Law of Water reveals that hydration is more than physical—it is an energetic tuning. Pure, intentional water brings vibrational harmony to the body, supporting healing, clarity, and sustained vitality.

Application:

How to Apply the Law of Water for Transcendent health and happiness...

Hydrate Your Body Consciously

Drink clean, living water throughout the day. Water nourishes organs, clears toxins, and fuels your energy field.

Bless your water. Speak words of gratitude or peace over it, acknowledging its sacred nature.

Flow with Life, Don't Resist It

When challenges arise, ask: *"How can I move through this like water?"*

Practice letting go rather than clinging. Water teaches that surrender is strength.

Connect with Water in Nature

Rivers, oceans, and rain all carry wisdom. Spend time near water to restore emotional balance and reconnect with Source.

Mindfulness Practice:

"Water Blessing Ritual"

1. Once daily, take a glass of water and hold it in your hands.

2. Silently or aloud, speak an intention over it, such as: "This water renews my body, calms my mind, and aligns my spirit."

3. Drink slowly, breathing deeply between sips. Visualize the water carrying healing energy throughout your body.

Final Thought:

*You are a living stream within the greater river of life. When you honor water—within and around you—you return to your natural state of **flow, harmony, and vitality**. By living in tune with the Law of Water, you align your body, heart, and spirit with the rhythm of the Earth and the wisdom of the Divine.*

Law of Physical Health #4:
The Law of Sunlight

Principle:
Gives the fire of life to the body along with vitamin D

The **Law of Sunlight** reveals that just as plants turn toward the sun for growth and life, **our bodies and souls also need the fire of light to thrive.** Sunlight is more than physical energy—it is a symbol of divine presence, clarity, and life force. Physically, sunlight provides essential vitamin D, regulates our circadian rhythms, boosts mood, and strengthens immunity. Spiritually, it awakens the inner fire—**the light of awareness, vitality, and joy**.

The sun represents **consciousness, strength, and radiant truth**. Living in harmony with this law means welcoming light—both literal and metaphorical—into your daily life. It reminds us to live **openly, energetically, and with warmth**, just as the sun gives without hesitation.

On the quantum level, sunlight is more than just light and heat—it is a powerful source of **coherent energy and information** that interacts directly with the energy fields of your physical vessel. Exposure to natural sunlight nourishes your cells and quantum energy system, infusing you with vitality and harmony. Beyond the physical, sunlight's **coherent vibrations resonate with your body's electromagnetic field**, promoting quantum coherence and enhancing cellular communication.

This energetic exchange boosts your life force, strengthens your immune system, and elevates your mood and mental clarity. By absorbing sunlight, you align with the universe's fundamental source of energy, igniting **tremendous vitality** from within!

Application:

How to Apply the Law of Sunlight for Transcendent health and happiness...

Receive Natural Sunlight Daily

Aim for 10-30 minutes of sunlight each day (preferably in the morning). Let it touch your skin, face, and eyes (safely). It nourishes your body and lifts your spirit.

Awaken Your Inner Light

Reflect on your gifts and passions—what makes you feel alive and bright? Cultivate and share that inner fire.

Cleanse with Light

Open your windows. Spend time in bright spaces. Let sunlight fill your home and thoughts with clarity and renewal.

Mindfulness Practice:

"Sunlight Gratitude Moment"

Each morning or evening, step outside and face the sun. Close your eyes. Take a deep breath and say silently or aloud:

"I receive the light of life. I shine with strength, joy, and purpose."

Feel the warmth filling your body and energizing your day or calming your evening.

Final Thought:

*The sun never withholds its light—and neither should you. By embracing the **Law of Sunlight**, you align with the sacred fire that sustains life, illuminates truth, and empowers your path. Let the outer light awaken your inner light, and walk in the radiance of who you truly are*

Law of Physical Health #5:
The Law of Temperance

Principle:
Temperance is harmony for a joyous life through perfect balance.
Balance in Moderation of eating those things which are healthy for us an abstinence in those things that are not healthy for us.

The **Law of Temperance** teaches that true health and harmony come from **moderation, balance, and self-control**. It is the principle of living wisely—avoiding excess, choosing what nourishes, and abstaining from what harms. When we practice temperance, we align with the natural rhythms of the body and soul, cultivating strength, clarity, and peace.

Temperance doesn't mean deprivation—it means **freedom through discipline**. It empowers you to say "yes" to what uplifts your well-being and "no" to habits that drain your energy or cloud your mind. This law reminds us that **vitality comes not only from what we take in, but also from what we choose to leave out.**

On the quantum level, your body and mind function as a finely tuned energy system. The **Law of Temperance** teaches that **moderation in good things and abstaining from harmful things** creates balance and coherence in your energetic field—supporting the optimal functioning of your physical vessel.

Excess—whether in food, stimulation, or behavior—creates **energetic chaos**, disrupting the natural rhythm of your body and lowering your vibration. On the other hand, **intentional moderation** promotes **quantum coherence**, where your cells, organs, and energy centers operate in harmony with each other and with the greater field of life.

Temperance is not restriction, but **wise regulation**—honoring the needs of the body while avoiding the energetic distortions caused by overindulgence or toxic habits. This balance preserves your life force and enhances clarity, vitality, and emotional stability.

So, on the quantum level, the Law of Temperance reveals: **balance in what you consume and how you live keeps your energy field clear and strong—allowing your physical vessel to thrive in alignment with universal harmony.**

Application:

How to Apply the Law of Temperance

1. **Eat and Drink Mindfully**
- Choose whole, nourishing foods and pure water. Avoid overindulgence and limit or eliminate harmful substances like processed sugar, alcohol, and artificial additives.

2. **Establish Gentle Boundaries**
- Practice moderation not just in diet, but in screen time, conversations, spending, and even work. Ask: *Is this bringing balance or imbalance?*

3. **Replace, Don't Just Remove**
- When abstaining from something unhealthful, replace it with something good—like herbal tea instead of soda, or a walk instead of passive scrolling.

Mindfulness Practice:

"The Temperance Pause"

Before eating, drinking, or engaging in any repeated activity, take a breath and ask:

"Will this bring life to my body and clarity to my mind?"

If yes—proceed with gratitude. If not—pause, and choose what honors your highest self.

Final Thought:

*Temperance is a gentle strength—**a form of love in action**. It protects your health, sharpens your mind, and honors your body as a temple. When you live by the Law of Temperance, you walk in wisdom, mastering your desires instead of being mastered by them, and creating space for peace, energy, and purpose to flourish.*

Law of Physical Health #6:
The Law of Air

Principle:
The Principle of deep breathing centers us in mindfulness and connects us with the Divine source, as spirit (ruach) is often likened to breath!

The **Law of Air** teaches that **breath is life**, and that air—both physical and spiritual—is our constant connection to the Source. In Scripture, the Spirit of God is often likened to **breath** (Hebrew *"ruach"*, Greek *"pneuma"*)—a gentle, unseen force that animates and sustains all living things. Every breath we take is a reminder that **God is near, within, and around us**, flowing through our lungs, minds, and hearts.

Physically, air is our most immediate need; we can live days without food or water, but only minutes without breath. Spiritually, conscious breathing awakens awareness, calms the nervous system, and opens us to divine presence. **To breathe deeply is to live deeply.**

On the quantum level, air is more than oxygen—it is life-force energy (prana, chi) that carries vibrational information and sustains your connection to the greater field of consciousness. The **Law of Air** teaches that **deep, conscious breathing** harmonizes your body's energy system, centers you in the present moment, and opens a channel to the Divine Source.

Every breath is an exchange of energy between your inner world and the quantum field. Shallow, unconscious breathing reflects disconnection and stress, creating energetic imbalance. But **slow, mindful breathing** calms the nervous system, aligns brainwave patterns, and generates **coherence in your electromagnetic field**, allowing higher states of awareness and peace to emerge.

Breath is the only autonomic function you can consciously control—making it a sacred tool for self-regulation and spiritual alignment. With each deep inhale, you receive life. With each exhale, you release resistance.

So, on the quantum level, the Law of Air reveals: breath is the energetic bridge between body, mind, and spirit. Conscious breathing aligns you with the Divine Source and brings your entire being into harmony with the present moment.

Application:

How to Apply the Law of Air for Transcendent health and happiness...

Practice Conscious Breathing

- Throughout the day, pause and take slow, deep breaths to center yourself. Breath is a sacred bridge between body and spirit.

Get Fresh, Clean Air

- Spend time outdoors in nature, ventilate your living spaces, and be mindful of the quality of air around you. Your body and soul thrive on purity.

Use Breath to Shift Energy

- In moments of stress or distraction, return to your breath. Inhale peace, exhale tension. Let your breath carry you back to stillness.

Mindfulness Practice:

"Spirit-Breath Meditation"
1. Sit quietly for 3–5 minutes and breathe deeply.

2. As you inhale, say inwardly:
   "The breath of God fills me."

3. As you exhale, say:
   "The peace of God flows through me."

   Repeat slowly, and allow each breath to soften your body and awaken your spirit.

Final Thought:

*Air is invisible, yet it gives life to everything. So it is with the Spirit—ever present, quietly sustaining, always flowing. When you live in harmony with the **Law of Air**, you become more aware, more present, and more aligned with the sacred rhythm of life itself.* ***Each breath becomes a prayer, and each moment, a gift.***

Law of Physical Health #7:
The Law of Regeneration through Rest

Principle:
Sleep is one of the most healing physiological principles.

The **Law of Regeneration through Rest** teaches that deep renewal—physically, mentally, and spiritually—comes when we allow the body and mind to **pause, replenish, and heal**. One of the most powerful and often overlooked healing forces is **sleep**. During sleep, the body repairs tissue, balances hormones, strengthens the immune system, and consolidates memory. Spiritually, rest creates a sacred space where the soul reconnects with divine harmony.

Just as the earth rests at night and the Sabbath offers a time for renewal, our bodies follow a natural rhythm of **activity and rest**. Ignoring rest leads to fatigue, anxiety, and burnout. Embracing rest restores energy, clarity, and emotional balance. It is through rest that we are **regenerated—made whole again**

On the quantum level, rest is not idleness—it is a powerful recalibration of your energy field. The Law of Regeneration through Rest teaches that true healing and restoration occur when the overactive lower mind (ego-mind) becomes still, allowing your energetic systems to **return to coherence and open to Higher frequencies**.

Just as meditation quiets mental noise and activates deeper brainwave states (like theta and delta), **intentional rest—whether sleep, silence, or stillness—slows down chaotic thought patterns**, which often vibrate at lower, fragmented frequencies. In this stillness, your cells, nervous system, and subtle energy fields begin to **repair, reorganize, and realign** with Source intelligence.

When the mind rests, the **superconscious and intuitive layers of your being become more accessible**, fostering spiritual insight, creativity, and emotional healing. This mirrors how in quantum physics, **potential collapses into form only in the presence of focused observation**—and rest creates the space for Higher awareness to flow in without interference.

So, on the quantum level, the Law of Regeneration through Rest reveals: stillness heals the fragmented lower mind and creates the energetic conditions for deep restoration, spiritual alignment, and connection to the Divine.

Key: *Getting 8 hours a night in a quiet dark room with clean fresh air and no electro magnetic interference from electron devices is one of the best ways to regenerate the body!*

Application:

How to Apply the Law of Rest for Transcendent health and happiness...

Prioritize Sleep

Aim for 7-9 hours of quality sleep per night. Create a calming bedtime routine—dim lights, avoid screens, and unwind with stillness.

Honor the Rhythms of Your Body

Listen to when your body needs rest—whether it's sleep, a nap, or a pause from mental strain. Don't push through exhaustion.

Practice Spiritual Stillness

Rest is not just physical—it's spiritual. Schedule moments of silence, prayer, or meditation throughout your day to restore inner peace.

Mindfulness Practice:

"Evening Restoration Ritual"

1. Before bed, sit or lie down comfortably.

2. Take a few deep breaths. Say inwardly or aloud: *"I release the day. I welcome healing rest."*

3. Visualize your body being bathed in peaceful light as you drift into sleep. Let your breath and trust in divine care carry you into restoration.

Final Thought:

Rest is not laziness or idleness—it is sacred wisdom. By living in harmony with the **Law of Regeneration through Rest***, you allow the natural forces of renewal to work within you.* ***In stillness, the body heals, the mind clears, and the spirit is strengthened.*** *Rest is a gift—and in receiving it, you honor both creation and the Creator.*

For all those other things you cannot control about your body or health Transcend by trusting in Divine power through prayer and meditation. These seven above laws along with "TRUST in Divine Power" comprise a beautiful acronym spelling NEW START, and that is exactly what gift you have been given. Each day you have the ability to start a new with the right principles for a healthy and happy body!

Chapter Summary/Key Takeaways

In summary, the 7 **Laws of Physical Health** are divine principles that govern the care and vitality of the body—our sacred vessel for life and spiritual expression. These laws are not merely about survival, but about thriving in harmony with nature and the Creator. They include:

1) **Nutrition:** Fuel your body with pure, whole foods that nourish and heal.

2) **Exercise:** Movement strengthens the body and energizes the mind—vitality flows through action.

3) **Water:** Stay hydrated; water cleanses, refreshes, and reflects the life-giving flow of Spirit.

4) **Sunlight:** Absorb the healing rays of the sun, a source of energy, clarity, and emotional balance.

5) **Temperance:** Live with moderation and self-control; avoid what harms, and choose what uplifts.

6) **Air:** Breathe deeply and seek fresh air—the breath of life that restores body and soul.

7) **Rest:** Honor your body's need for sleep and stillness; regeneration happens in quiet renewal.

8) **Trust in Divine Power:** Health flourishes when grounded in faith. Trusting in God brings peace, resilience, and purpose.

By aligning with these timeless laws every day and in every situation, we respect the divine design of the human body and open ourselves to physical vitality, emotional balance, and spiritual clarity. Living in this way brings harmony, allows healing and is a daily act of worship and wisdom.

Coming Up Next...
Now that we understand the value of caring for our physical temple, we turn to the equally vital practice of **cultivating healthy, life-giving relationships**—the heart's true environment for growth, joy, and spiritual maturity! Just as the body thrives when cared for through proper nourishment, movement, rest, and connection to the divine, **so too does the soul flourish through healthy, loving relationships...** In the next chapter you will learn about the seven Laws of Relationship Health!

CHAPTER FIVE:
The 7 Laws of Relationship Health

Healthy, meaningful relationships are **essential to a whole and spiritually rooted life**. Just as our physical bodies require care and balance, so do our relationships. They are the sacred spaces where we learn to love, grow, and reflect the divine presence in one another. Whether with partners, family, friends, or community, every connection we nurture carries the potential to **heal, empower, and transform**.

The **7 Laws of Relationship Health** are timeless principles that guide us in creating and sustaining relationships that are life-giving and spiritually aligned. Each law invites us to shift our focus inward as well as outward—recognizing that the quality of our connections often mirrors the quality of our inner state.

These seven laws are:

1. **The Law of Equality** – True relationships are rooted in mutual respect and shared value, where each person's voice and worth are equally honored.

2. **The Law of Mirror Reflection** – Others reflect aspects of ourselves; our relationships become powerful teachers if we are willing to see clearly.

3. **The Law of Change** – People evolve, and so must our relationships. Openness to growth allows love to deepen and adapt over time.

4. **The Law of Mindfulness in the Present Moment** – Presence is the greatest gift we can give. Real connection happens only in the now.

5. **The Law of Letting Go of Being Right** – Peace in relationships often comes not from winning, but from surrendering pride for understanding.

6. **The Law of Feeding Relationships** – Love, like anything living, must be nourished—through time, attention, gratitude, and care.

7. **The Law of Healthy Communication** – Honest, compassionate communication is the bridge between hearts; it creates clarity, trust, and intimacy.

Together, these laws form a spiritual and emotional blueprint for **deepening connection, healing wounds, and building relationships that reflect the love and wisdom of the Divine.** As we learn to live by them, our relationships become not only stronger—but more sacred. Now let's go deeper into each law and how to apply them...

Law of Relationship Health #1:
The Law of Equality

Principle:
We all are different expressions of the same underlying spirit and therefore are equal!

Although people have different genders and roles and purposes in their life at a core level we are all equal as we are all Sparks of the divine flame and must recognize that divinity in each other and treat it with dignity and honor and love. Love is the great Unity as all come from Love! The **Law of Equality** teaches that all individuals have equal worth, value, and dignity, regardless of roles, background, or personality differences. In relationships, this law reminds us that true connection can only thrive when both people are respected as equals. Power imbalances, judgment, or control erode trust, while mutual respect and shared responsibility foster harmony, safety, and growth.

When we embrace equality, we listen without domination, speak without fear, and honor one another's feelings, needs, and contributions. This law benefits our relationships by encouraging fairness, empathy, and collaboration—laying the foundation for deep, lasting bonds.

On a spiritual level we are all a part of the Divine Source and so we must remember that however we treat others is how we are treating "God", and this is why the scripture says, "...in as much as you have done to one of the least of these people, you have done to Me" -

On the quantum level, all particles—and by extension, all beings—are fundamentally interconnected and equally valued parts of the same energetic field. The **Law of Equality** reflects this truth: no energy is superior or inferior; it simply expresses differently within the unified field.

In the context of **relationship health,** this law teaches that **each person is energetically sovereign yet intrinsically equal.** When we recognize the quantum reality that every being carries the same Source essence, we naturally shift into relationships rooted in **mutual respect, compassion, and dignity.**

Energetically, when equality is practiced, relationships move out of power struggles and emotional imbalances, and into **coherence,** a state where energies align and resonate in harmony. Just as balanced particles interact without domination or depletion, **balanced relationships thrive when both individuals are valued and heard.**

Thus, the **Law of Equality enhances relationship health** by encouraging us to honor the divine spark in ourselves and others, fostering deeper connection, emotional safety, and sacred partnership.

Application:

How to Apply the Law of Equality in your Life...

- Treat every person as worthy of respect and kindness, regardless of status or opinion.
- Release superiority or inferiority complexes and practice seeing others through the eyes of love and dignity realizing all is a part of the All in All.
- Share decision-making and emotional labor in relationships; listen as much as you speak.

Mindfulness Practice:

Practice **"Equal Listening"**:

1. In a conversation with a friend, partner, or coworker, spend 5 minutes listening **without interrupting**, correcting, or offering advice.

2. Simply reflect what they've said and express appreciation for their perspective. Notice how this deepens your connection and reinforces the law of equality.

Final Thought:

When we honor the Law of Equality, we create relationships built on mutual respect, trust, and emotional safety. No one is diminished, and no one dominates. Instead, each person is seen, heard, and valued for who they truly are. This balance allows love to flow freely, reduces conflict born of ego or control, and nurtures a sense of shared purpose. In this space of equality, relationships flourish—becoming healthier, more joyful, and deeply fulfilling for everyone involved.

Law of Relationship Health #2:
The Law of Mirror Reflection

Principle:
Our relationships are mirrors of ourself... our "inner" self!

The Law of Mirror Reflection teaches that the people we attract and the relationships we experience are reflections of our own inner world— our beliefs, emotions, and unresolved patterns. What we admire or resent in others often points to what we either possess or need to heal within ourselves. Understanding this law helps us move from blame to self-awareness, seeing each relationship as an opportunity for growth and transformation.

Relationships mirror back to you how you are feeling inside and what energy you are giving off. You can't look in the mirror and frown and have the mirror smile; it is impossible. This is the same way relationships work. The ancient law "As above, so below, as within, so without, as the universe, so the soul..." reflects that "As Within" - (*What do we think within ourselves*) "So Without" – (*Will be expressed or reflected on the world we live*).

This reveals that we must recognize God is trying to reveal things to us through the other person and so we must not resent or resist something we do not like in someone else but receive it as a mirror of an area in our life we need to correct. We must be the kind of person we want to attract!

On the quantum level, the universe operates through resonance—**like frequencies attract and reflect one another...** and in the context of our relationships we find that the people and situations we encounter in our external world often reflect our **internal beliefs, emotional patterns, and self-perception.**

In relationships, this means that others act as **mirrors**, revealing aspects of our **inner self**—both conscious and unconscious. If we attract love, trust, or kindness, it often reflects the presence of those qualities within us. If we experience conflict, fear, or rejection, it may point to **unhealed emotions or limiting beliefs** we hold inside.

Quantum physics supports this with the idea that the **observer affects the observed**—our inner state subtly shapes what we perceive and experience. By recognizing this mirror effect, we can stop blaming others and instead **use every relationship as a tool for self-awareness and transformation.**

Thus, the Law of Mirror Reflection invites us to look within, **heal what's unbalanced**, and embody the love and peace we wish to see—because what is within, will be reflected without.

Application:

How to Apply the Law of Mirrored Reflections in your Life...

> When triggered or inspired by someone, pause and reflect: *What in me is being revealed?*
>
> Instead of reacting outwardly, look inward.
> This awareness allows you to respond with compassion and clarity, rather than defensiveness or judgment.

Mindfulness Practice:

Choose one challenging interaction from your day.

Journal:

1. What emotions came up?

2. What does this situation reflect about my own patterns or inner beliefs?

3. What would healing or growth look like in this area?

Consistently using this mirror helps you deepen self-understanding and cultivate healthier, more authentic relationships.

Final Thought:

The great epiphany of the Law of Mirror Reflection is this: every relationship is a sacred opportunity for self-awareness and transformation. When we realize that what we admire—or resist—in others often reveals something about ourselves, we stop blaming and start learning. Others become mirrors, not enemies or saviors, but reflections guiding us back to our own hearts. In seeing them more clearly, we begin to truly see ourselves—and that is where healing begins.

Law of Relationship Health #3:
The Law of Change

Principle:
Relationships are for change... and change is good! Relationships are meant to encourage selflessness and growth, and Selfless love recreates us in God's image!

The Law of Change teaches that growth and change are constant, natural parts of life—and this includes our relationships. People evolve, circumstances shift, and relationships must adapt to remain healthy. Resisting change can create conflict or stagnation, while embracing it allows relationships to mature, deepen, or release when necessary. Change isn't something to fear; it's a vital ingredient in love, connection, and shared growth.

When we cling sentimentally to things remaining the same, we invite unnecessary suffering into our lives. The illusion that things should remain the same denies the very nature of life itself—impermanence. Everything is in motion: people grow, values shift, and seasons of life come and go. By attaching ourselves to static expectations, we create emotional resistance to the flow of life. This resistance often leads to grief, anxiety, or disillusionment. But when we surrender to the rhythm of change, we discover peace. We learn to love in the present, appreciate what was, and trust what's becoming. In this acceptance, we gain the freedom to grow with grace.

On the quantum level, everything in the universe is in constant motion—**energy is never static, but always evolving**. The **Law of Change** aligns with this principle, showing us that transformation is a fundamental part of existence.

In relationships, this means that no connection remains the same. People grow, emotions shift, and dynamics evolve. When we resist this natural flow, we create energetic tension. But when we **embrace change as a catalyst for growth**, our relationships become powerful mirrors and vehicles for inner development.

Quantum physics reveals that **possibility exists in every moment**—a field of potential waiting to be shaped by our choices and awareness. Being flexible in relationships allows us to tune into this field, **adapting with compassion, learning new perspectives, and expanding our capacity to love.**
Thus, the Law of Change reminds us that relationships are not meant to stay fixed—they are sacred invitations to **grow, evolve, and co-create something higher than either person alone.**

Application:

How to Embrace the Law of Change rather than resisting it...

Recognize that change is not a threat but an invitation. Allow space for your partner, friend, or loved one to grow and change—just as you are growing too. Commit to open, compassionate communication when transitions occur, and stay curious rather than judgmental.

Mindfulness Practice:

Reflect on a recent change in a relationship...

Ask:
1. What am I learning through this change?
2. How can I support both myself and the other person during this transition?
3. What would letting go of control look like here?

Final Thought:

When we stop resisting change and start flowing with it, relationships become more resilient, alive, and meaningful. Growth—individually and together—is the heart of love.

Law of Relationship Health #4:
The Law of Mindfulness

Principle:
Relationships thrive in the Present Moment, not the Past! The Past does not exist... All we have is the Present Moment!

No bringing up the past or speaking a critical word about the past. Philippians 3:13 says, "Forgetting what lies behind and straining forward to what lies ahead."

The **Law of Mindfulness** teaches that being fully present in each moment is one of the most powerful gifts we can offer in our relationships. When we are truly mindful—listening without distraction, responding without reactivity, and being aware of our emotions and thoughts—we create a space for deeper connection, empathy, and understanding. Mindfulness helps us break patterns of unconscious behavior, reduces miscommunication, and allows us to meet others with genuine presence and compassion.

On the quantum level, time is not fixed—**past, present, and future are fluid possibilities** within the field of energy. What gives reality its shape is **our focused attention in the now.** The **Law of Mindfulness** aligns with this principle by emphasizing that true connection, healing, and transformation can only happen in the **present moment.**

In relationships, clinging to the past or projecting into the future distorts the energy we share. But when we are fully present—with open awareness and non-judgment—we **collapse the infinite quantum possibilities into meaningful connection** right now. Presence is power.

Mindfulness tunes us into the vibrational field of love, empathy, and clarity. It allows us to **respond instead of react**, to **see others as they truly are**, and to nurture relationships in real time. Since the past is merely a mental construct and the future is unrealized potential, **the only point of creation is now**.

Therefore, on the quantum level, **mindfulness aligns our relationships with the Source field of unity and potential**, making the present moment the only place where love can truly live and thrive.

Application:

How to Apply the Law of Mindfulness to your relationships...

Practice being fully present during interactions. This means putting away distractions, making eye contact, and tuning into both your own internal state and the emotions of the person you're with. Mindfulness also involves noticing when your mind drifts into past hurts or future worries, and gently returning your attention to the now.

Mindfulness Practice:

1. Each day, choose one conversation to approach mindfully.

2. Take a few deep breaths before engaging, listen actively without thinking about what you are going to say or interrupting, and notice your internal reactions without immediately expressing them.

3. Reflect afterward: how did mindfulness shift the dynamic?

Final Thought:

Mindfulness transforms ordinary moments into sacred exchanges. By simply showing up fully—without judgment or agenda—we invite others to do the same. In this still, attentive presence, love can be heard more clearly, trust can take root, and healing can begin.

Law of Relationship Health #5:
The Law of Relinquishing being Right!

Principle:
We must seek to understand the other person's perspectives and choose to show kindness and maintain the peace and love rather than arguing over who is "right".

The **Law of Relinquishing Being Right** emphasizes that in relationships, the need to be "right" often comes at the expense of peace, connection, and love. When we insist on proving a point, winning an argument, or correcting others, we can unintentionally damage trust and intimacy. Prioritizing happiness means choosing harmony, mutual respect, and emotional well-being over the ego's need to win. It's not about suppressing truth, but about valuing kindness and understanding more than control or superiority.

On the quantum level, reality is not fixed but shaped by **vibration, intention, and observation**. When we cling to the need to be "right," we lock our consciousness into a lower vibrational state—rooted in **ego, resistance, and separation**. This creates disharmony in our personal energy field and distorts the relational field between ourselves and others.

The **Law of Relinquishing Being Right** invites us to shift from the ego's illusion of control to the soul's truth of connection. In quantum terms, this act of surrender **collapses the wave of conflict into a particle of peace**—allowing love, unity, and understanding to emerge. The energy of humility and openness aligns us with the quantum field's higher frequencies, where **coherence and compassion override division**.

When we release the need to "win" an argument or prove ourselves, we free our energy to resonate with the **higher field of Oneness,** where authentic relationships can grow. In this way, letting go of being right becomes not a loss, but a quantum leap into deeper harmony and love.

This is a paradigm shift in alignment with the power of positive thinking! But to truly live out this law we must clearly see that it is more important to choose happiness and peace in all things rather than pushing our points verbally to prove to be "right".

Application:

How to Apply this Law in your Relationships...

Next time a disagreement arises, pause and ask yourself: *Is it more important to be right, or to be loving and connected?*

Choose your words and responses in a way that fosters peace and love and rather than division. Let go of the need to have the last word or to prove yourself. In doing so, you allow room for dialogue, not debate.

Mindfulness Practice:

1. Practice letting go in small moments: if someone makes a minor mistake or has a different opinion, resist the urge to correct or challenge them.

2. Instead, listen with curiosity and respond with grace.

3. Keep a journal noting how choosing happiness over being right affected the outcome of a conversation.

Final Thought:

True wisdom lies in knowing that peace is more powerful than pride. In choosing happiness over being right, we affirm that relationships are not battles to win, but sacred spaces to grow, love, and understand each other. In those moments of surrender, we often discover deeper truths— and a deeper connection.

Law of Relationship Health #6:
The Law of Feeding your Relationships

Principle:
We must feed and nurture our relationships with Attention, Affection, Appreciation, and our Time!

From both Spiritual wisdom as well as scientific law, we learn that everything is energy—including our thoughts, emotions, and relationships. The **Law of Feeding Our Relationships** reflects the principle that **where we place our attention and intention, energy flows and grows.**

Just as subatomic particles respond to observation, our relationships respond to the **energetic focus** we give them. When we offer love, presence, gratitude, and care, we infuse the relational field with high-vibrational energy that fosters connection and trust. This energetic investment creates a **resonant field of coherence**, strengthening the invisible bonds between us.

Conversely, neglect or emotional absence weakens the energetic structure, leading to disconnection. **Quantumly speaking, we're either reinforcing or diminishing the relational energy field with every interaction.**

Feeding our relationships, then, is a conscious act of **energetic nurturing**—aligning our intentions and emotions to create thriving, resonant, and loving connections that mirror the interconnectedness of all life.

Relationships have often been likened to a garden producing according to the attention given it. The Law of Feeding Your Relationships teaches that just like a garden needs attentive care and regular maintenance to thrive, relationships need consistent care, attention, and positive energy to stay healthy and strong.

Love, appreciation, quality time, and meaningful connection are the "food" that sustains emotional bonds and the "fertilizer" to help them grow stronger. Neglect, busyness, or taking others for granted can weaken even the strongest relationships over time.

Feeding a relationship is an act of intention—it requires presence, effort, and love expressed in action and requires consistent nourishment through four essential elements:

Attention,
Affection,
Appreciation,
and **Time**

These are the daily investments that communicate love, value, and presence. When we give someone our focused attention, express genuine affection, speak words of appreciation, and share our time generously, we strengthen the emotional bond. Neglecting these areas can lead to emotional distance, but intentional care breathes life into any connection.

Application:

How to Apply the **Law of Mindfulness** in your Relationships: Become more mindful of these four pillars in your relationships. Ask yourself daily: *Have I truly seen, touched, thanked, and spent meaningful time with those I care about today?* This awareness turns everyday interactions into moments of connection and emotional nourishment.

- **Attention...** In person focus and interaction...
- **Affection...** Affection through smiles, acts of kindness, and kind words before touch.

- **Appreciation...** Share the things you appreciate about the other person
- **Time...** Give of your time in sharing what the other person is interested in

Mindfulness Practice:

Choose one person in your life. Each day for the next week, intentionally express:

1. **Attention** by listening without distractions,
2. **Affection** through kindness and/or words,
3. **Appreciation** by voicing something you value about them,
4. and **Time** by being fully present with them, even for just a few minutes.

Keep a journal of how this practice affects your relationship and your own emotional state.

Final Thought:

*Love doesn't just survive on good intentions—it thrives on **daily attention, affection, appreciation, and time.** These simple but powerful gifts are the nutrients of a healthy relationship. When we feed what matters, we don't just build stronger connections—we become more loving, fulfilled versions of ourselves.*

Law of Relationship Health #7:
The Law of Communication

Principle:
Communication is essential for any relationship, so we must learn to communicate in only healthy ways... as well as know the importance of being a good listener!

The Law of Communication states that clear, honest, and respectful exchange of thoughts and feelings is essential for building and maintaining healthy relationships. Whether in friendships, family, or work, effective communication fosters understanding, trust, and connection. Without it, misunderstandings grow, conflicts escalate, and relationships suffer.

On a quantum level, everything in existence is in a constant state of **communication**—exchanging information through vibrations, frequencies, and energy fields. Particles "speak" across time and space through quantum entanglement, where a change in one instantly affects the other, regardless of distance. This reveals a deep **interconnected intelligence** built into the fabric of reality.

In this way, the **Law of Communication** reflects the universal truth that **all things are relational**. Whether between atoms, cells, ecosystems, or people, **clear communication sustains harmony, coherence, and balance**. Just as subatomic particles respond to energy and intention, human relationships flourish when we share truthfully, listen deeply, and transmit love.

When we consciously align our words and intentions with the frequency of love and truth, we join the cosmic conversation—participating in the divine rhythm that keeps the universe in perfect, living order. Communication, then, is not just practical—it is **sacred**, and a quantum tool for unity and healing.

Why It's Essential:
Healthy relationships thrive on open dialogue where both parties feel heard and valued. Communication bridges gaps between differing perspectives, resolves conflicts peacefully, and deepens emotional bonds. It is the foundation that allows love, respect, and cooperation to flourish. So we must engage in more listening than speaking... for as they say, "God created us with two ears and only one mouth, therefore we should be listening more than speaking"!

Application:

How to Apply the **Law of Communication** in Your Relationships...

- Practice active listening: focus fully on the speaker without interrupting or planning your response.

- Express your thoughts clearly and kindly, using "I" statements to own your feelings rather than blaming others.

- Be honest but compassionate, sharing your needs and concerns without judgment.

- Check for understanding by asking clarifying questions and summarizing what you heard.

Mindfulness Practice:

1. Each day, try a "communication check-in" with someone close to you.
2. Take a few minutes to genuinely ask how they're feeling and share how you're doing.
3. Use this time to listen deeply and speak openly, strengthening your connection through intentional communication.

Final Thought:

Communication is more than just words—it's the bridge that connects hearts and minds. By embracing this law, you nurture relationships that grow stronger through honesty, empathy, and mutual respect. The effort you put into communicating well today will blossom into lasting bonds tomorrow.

Chapter Summary/Key Takeaways

In summary, we are created for relationship and so it is so important to apply these 7 Laws of Relational Health in every area of your life with your parents, spouse, children, friends and the people you work with as these laws form a spiritual and emotional blueprint for **deepening our connections, healing wounds, and building up relationships that reflect the love and wisdom of the Divine!**

1) **The Law of Equality** – True relationships are rooted in mutual respect and shared value, where each person's voice and worth are equally honored.

2) **The Law of Mirror Reflection** – Others reflect aspects of ourselves; our relationships become powerful teachers if we are willing to see clearly.

3) **The Law of Change** – People evolve, and so must our relationships. Openness to growth allows love to deepen and adapt over time.

4) **The Law of Mindfulness in the Present Moment** – Presence is the greatest gift we can give. Real connection happens only in the now.

5) **The Law of Letting Go of Being Right** – Peace in relationships often comes not from winning, but from surrendering pride for understanding.

6) **The Law of Feeding Relationships** – Love, like anything living, must be nourished—through time, attention, gratitude, and care.

7) **The Law of Healthy Communication** – Honest, compassionate communication is the bridge between hearts; it creates clarity, trust, and intimacy.

Coming Up Next...
Once we realize how important others are, then we can seek abundance for the greater good. Just as our relationships thrive when we honor the laws that govern connection, trust, and communication, so too does our financial well-being flourish when we align with the **spiritual and practical principles of abundance**.

In the next chapter you will learn about the seven Laws of Financial Health and Attracting Abundance!

CHAPTER SIX:
The 7 Laws of Financial Health and Attracting Abundance

Financial health is much more than just numbers in a bank account—it is a holistic state of balance, freedom, and confidence in managing your resources. Just like physical health requires certain habits and principles, financial well-being is guided by key laws that, when understood and applied, empower you to attract abundance and create lasting prosperity.

The **7 Laws of Financial Health** are foundational principles that help you align your mindset, habits, and decisions with the flow of wealth. These laws reveal how to manage money wisely, grow it intentionally, and cultivate a positive relationship with abundance. By embracing these laws, you open the door to financial stability and the freedom to live a life of purpose and generosity.

In this journey, attracting abundance is not about luck or wishful thinking—it's about practical steps, intentional actions, and shifting your mindset to welcome opportunities and prosperity. Understanding these laws will equip you with the tools to overcome financial challenges, break limiting patterns, and build a foundation for wealth that lasts.

Get ready to explore these transformative laws and discover how you can create a life of financial health and abundant blessings.

Law of Financial Health #1:
The Law of Realizing your Oneness with the Source of all Resource!

Principle:
"I AM the Source of all Resources needed."

The Law of Oneness with the Source of All Resource teaches that everything—wealth, opportunities, and blessings—flows from one infinite Source. When we understand that we are deeply connected to this Source and to each other, we realize that abundance is unlimited and accessible to all. This awareness dissolves scarcity mindsets and opens our hearts to receive and share generously.

How Understanding Attracts Abundance:

By recognizing this Oneness with the Source, we align ourselves with the natural flow of abundance rather than trying to grasp or control limited resources. This alignment fosters trust, peace, and a sense of unity that draws prosperity effortlessly. Abundance becomes not just about personal gain but about uplifting others and contributing to the greater good.

The "I AM" principle of our true Divine identity realizes it is connected to the Divine Source and thereby has access to all the resources necessary for whatever good one wants to be a conduit of as an extension of the Divine Source.

At the quantum level, all matter and energy arise from the same **unified field**—a limitless source from which everything is continually created and sustained. When you recognize your **oneness** with this Source, you stop perceiving life through the lens of scarcity and competition, and instead align with the **natural flow of abundance.**

In quantum terms, your inner state of trust and receptivity influences the wave of infinite possibilities, drawing to you the resources that match your vibration. Rather than grasping or controlling what you think is "limited," you become a cooperative participant in the universe's self-sustaining cycle, where **giving and receiving are in constant balance.**

This realization transforms lack into sufficiency—not by force, but by resonance—allowing abundance to manifest as naturally as sunlight flows through space.

Application:

How to Apply This **Law of Oneness with the Source of all Resource** in your Life...

- Cultivate a mindset of connection, seeing yourself as part of a greater whole rather than isolated.

- Practice gratitude daily for the resources you have, acknowledging the Source behind all blessings.

- Use your resources—time, money, talents—not only for yourself but to help and empower others.

- Trust that by giving freely, you are participating in the endless cycle of abundance.

Mindfulness Practice:

Each day, engage in a simple reflection: "How can I be a channel of abundance today?" Whether through a kind word, sharing your skills, or giving financially, act with the intention of serving the greater good.

Notice how this shift in focus transforms your experience of abundance. The principle of the Universe is such that the more we give, the more we receive... and likewise the more we internalize that we have everything we need and we are a part of the All in All, we will naturally attract that same energy!

Final Thought:

True abundance flows when we embrace our oneness with the Source and live with generosity and purpose. By attracting wealth not just for ourselves but for the collective good, we create a world where prosperity is shared, and everyone thrives. Remember, abundance multiplied by unity becomes limitless.

Law of Financial Health #2:
The Law of Thinking, Believing & Feeling

Principle:
"Think and believe and feel what you want to attract as if it is already yours."

The Law of Thinking, Believing & Feeling reveals that the thoughts we hold, the beliefs we nurture, and the emotions we embody create the energetic foundation for what we attract in life. To draw abundance, we must think, believe, and feel as if the prosperity we desire is already ours. This alignment sends a powerful signal to the universe, opening doors and opportunities that match our inner state.

On the quantum level, reality exists as a field of infinite probabilities, with your **thoughts, beliefs, and feelings** acting like tuning forks that select which potentials collapse into your experience. When you not only think about something, but **believe** it is possible and **feel** it as though it is already yours, you create a coherent vibration that resonates with that specific outcome in the quantum field.

This inner congruence—thought aligned with belief, and belief infused with feeling—sends a clear "signal" into the fabric of reality, drawing matching experiences toward you. It's not wishful thinking; it's **energetic alignment**. In essence, you don't chase what you desire—you magnetize it by embodying it internally first, allowing the outer world to mirror your inner certainty.

How This Law Attracts Abundance:
When you consistently think positive thoughts, truly believe in your worthiness, and feel the joy and gratitude of already having abundance, you align your energy with your goals. This harmony

magnetizes resources and blessings not only for personal benefit but also for meaningful contribution to others. The power lies in living the reality of abundance now, which shifts your vibration and brings your desires into manifestation.

You must have a vision detailed like a blueprint and see it as already accomplished with the knowledge of every aspect of that vision and what it will take to see it manifested just like a builder or architect prepares before actually constructing a building. Some people only *think about* what they want but without connecting the *mind* to the *feelings and emotions* of the heart one will not see it come to full fruition as the heart and mind must be connected to see the power in prayer or the manifesting in the physical world from the spiritual world. This can be done throughout the day but the optimal time for visualizing with conviction and feeling goes back to the fifth law of Mental Mastery in chapter 2 concerning the Law of Attraction which reveals that visualizing what you want to attract just before you go to sleep is most powerful as it is then you are most closely connecting with the subconscious mind which is connected to the Divine Universal Mind which is in control of bringing all things into being.

Application:

How to Apply This **Law of Thinking, Believing & Feeling** in Your Life...

- Cultivate clear, positive thoughts about wealth and generosity daily.
- Affirm your belief in your ability to attract and share abundance.
- Feel the emotions of gratitude, joy, and fulfillment as if your goals are already achieved.

- Focus your mindset on abundance that supports not only yourself but also the well-being of your community and the greater good.

Mindfulness Practice:

1. Create a daily ritual of visualization combined with feeling.

2. Spend a few minutes imagining your life with abundant resources and the impact your generosity has on others.

3. Feel the gratitude and happiness of this reality deeply, reinforcing the belief that it is already yours and shared widely.

Final Thought:

Your thoughts, beliefs, and feelings are the seeds of your reality. By nurturing them with intention and purpose—aimed at abundance for all—you become a powerful creator of prosperity that uplifts yourself and the world around you. Remember, true abundance grows when it is shared from a heart aligned with unity and love.

Law of Financial Health #3:
The Law of Speaking only Good into Existence

Principle:
"Speak what you want to attract or manifest into existence."

The scriptures tell us that God spoke at Creation... and "it was Good". Just as the Divine Source thinks about what it wants to create and then speaks it into existence so must we as Co-creators with the Divine Creator. We must go beyond simply asking for things in prayer but claiming God's promises for our lives and speaking them into existence. God says through the Prophet Jeremiah "I know the plans I have for you plans to prosper you and do you good, plans to give you hope and a future.." (Jeremiah 29:11) Thus we must speak what we want to see come into existence and that speech must only be good speech and for the greater good for it to be blessed.

The opposite side of this coin is that we must not speak any doubt or negativity into existence as we only apply the law of speaking that which is good into existence. we must not doubt our inability or lack of giftings or talents but simply act by faith in the direction we are lead to accomplish are good purpose in this world and we will be blessed.

The **Law of Only Speaking Good into Existence** teaches that our words carry creative power. What we consistently speak, we give life to—whether good or bad. If we desire abundance, peace, and purpose, we must speak words that align with those outcomes. Negative talk—about ourselves, others, or our circumstances—only reinforces lack and limitation. But when we choose to speak positively and intentionally, we partner with the Source to manifest blessings into existence.

On the quantum level, words are not just sounds—they are **vibrational codes of energy** that influence the field of possibilities. Every time you speak, you send waves of energy into the quantum field, shaping the patterns that reality will mirror back to you. Speaking only what is good, uplifting, and aligned with what you desire focuses your vibration toward creation rather than destruction.

How This Law Attracts Abundance:

When you speak blessings, gratitude, and positive expectation, you reinforce the frequency of those outcomes, making them more likely to collapse into your lived experience. In this way, your tongue becomes a tool of manifestation—planting seeds in the unseen that grow into the reality you experience.

Thus, speaking faith-filled, encouraging, and grateful words lifts your vibration and aligns your environment with abundance. When your speech reflects trust in divine provision and your desire to bless others, you become a magnet for opportunities and overflow that serve not just you, but the greater good!

Application:

How to Apply This Law of Speaking only Good in Your Life...

- Be mindful of your speech; avoid complaining, gossiping, or self-defeating language.
- Replace negative statements with positive declarations rooted in truth and purpose.
- Speak affirmations that reflect the abundance you desire and your intention to use it to uplift others.
- Surround yourself with people and environments that encourage life-giving speech.

Mindfulness Practice:

Try a "Speech Fast" for 24 hours:

1. Commit to speaking only what is positive, hopeful, and aligned with what you want to create. If a negative thought arises, pause, reframe it, and speak a word of gratitude or faith instead.

2. Repeat this practice regularly to train your mind and mouth to co-create wisely.

Final Thought:

Your words are seeds—what you plant with your tongue will grow in your life. Speak life, speak abundance, speak goodness—not only for yourself but for the world you're shaping with every word. When your voice becomes a channel for light and love, you help manifest a better future for all.

Law of Financial Health #4:
The Law of Action

Principle:
"All positive thoughts are followed by positive speech and must be followed by positive action to manifest the desired result."

This is why the Zoroastrian religion of the ancient Persians is so powerful in that there main mantra is **"Good Thoughts, Good Words , Good Deeds"** which they learn from the Jewish exiles living among them who had learn these principles from Torah. The **Law of Action** declares that for any desire or intention to manifest, it must be followed by purposeful, aligned action. Positive thoughts and words alone are not enough—they must be carried into motion. This law reminds us that faith without works is incomplete. When our actions align with our intentions and values, we become powerful agents of change and abundance.

On the quantum level, thought and speech set energy in motion, but **action is what collapses potential into reality**. Positive thoughts generate a vibrational blueprint, positive speech amplifies and programs that blueprint, and positive action gives it physical form. Without action, the wave of possibility remains unobserved—never crystallizing into the tangible world.

When your deeds align with your highest intentions and words, you send a coherent signal to the quantum field, declaring, *"This is real now."* This alignment bridges the unseen and the seen, ensuring your desired result manifests in harmony with universal law.

How This Law Attracts Abundance:
Abundance flows not just to those who think or speak about it, but to those who act in accordance with it. When you take steps—no matter how small—toward your goals with faith, integrity, and

generosity, you invite momentum, open doors, and attract opportunities. Action becomes the bridge between your inner vision and outward reality, especially when that vision serves others and not just yourself.

Further insight into the Law of Action reveals that we must also understanding being in harmony with God's perfect order and timing... Thus,

Take the right ACTION,
in the right ORDER,
at the right TIME

Application:

How to Apply This Law of Action in Your Life...

- Turn positive thoughts and affirmations into specific, consistent action steps.

- Let your actions reflect your belief in abundance, showing up fully and responsibly.

- Act in ways that bless others—volunteer, give, create, or support initiatives that bring collective good.

- Avoid procrastination by breaking large goals into small, daily actions that align with your vision.

Mindfulness Practice:

Each morning, write down one positive intention and one practical action you will take to support it.

For example: *Intention: I live in financial peace. Action: I will track my spending today and give generously.*

Repeat this daily to build alignment between your mindset and movement.

Final Thought:

*Your actions are your declaration to the universe that you're ready to receive and steward abundance. When you move with purpose, integrity, and love—not just for yourself but for others—you activate the flow of blessings. Remember: **right thoughts, right words, and right actions together unlock divine results.***

*So **Think, Believe & Act** to Achieve... BUT according to the principle of the Universe which is selfless love – to get, you must also **GIVE a VALUE added SERVICE**. Which leads us into understanding the next law - that we must seek to manifest not for the self alone but for the greater good!*

Law of Financial Health #5:
The Law of Receiving not for the Self alone but for the Greater Good

Principle:
"Whatever we wish to manifest must be in harmony with the will of God and for the good of others"

Seek ye first the Kingdom of God and His righteousness and *then* all these things will be added unto you" (Matthew 6:33). **The law of life and love is always "other-centered"** and therefore to live in harmony with it and to be blessed by it we must apply the law to what we seek to manifest so that we can be a conduit of blessing to others and thereby the cycle of receiving will continue as we continue to give… just as there is a principle that the more you give the more you will receive.

The **Law of Receiving Abundance Not for the Self Alone but for the Greater Good** teaches that true abundance is not meant to be hoarded—it is entrusted to us for a higher purpose. Whatever we desire to manifest must be in harmony with the will of God and aligned with love, justice, and service to others. When our motives are pure and our hearts are set on lifting others, we become vessels through which divine provision flows freely.

How This Law Attracts Abundance:
God is the ultimate Source of all resources, and He blesses us not just for personal comfort but to equip us to meet needs, heal brokenness, and serve our communities. When we seek abundance with the intention to give, to build, and to bless, we come into alignment with Heaven's economy. This attracts not just material wealth, but favor, opportunity, and spiritual richness.

On the quantum level, reality is fundamentally interconnected. Particles influence one another instantly across space (which scientists call "quantum entanglement"), and they have found that observation itself alters outcomes (called "the observer effect"). These principles suggest that consciousness and intention matter at the deepest levels of existence.

When one acts to *receive not for the self alone*, but for the greater good, this intention aligns with the quantum field's tendency toward coherence, connection, and unity. Selfless receiving—motivated by love, service, and shared upliftment—generates a vibrational frequency that resonates with the quantum field's holistic nature.

This alignment creates a feedback loop: the more we receive in order to give, the more the universe responds with abundance, synchronicity, and flow. In contrast, selfish receiving creates energetic dissonance, limiting the flow of blessings. Thus, on a quantum level, giving and receiving become inseparable, and the universe supports those who participate in its interconnected harmony.

In short: **when you receive in order to bless others, you become a conductor of quantum coherence—and the field gives more to those who give more.**

Application:

How to Apply This **Law of Receiving Abundance Not for the Self Alone but for the Greater Good** in Your Life...

- Regularly check your motives: ask yourself, "Is what I'm asking for meant to glorify God and help others?"

- When setting goals or asking for provision, include how it will be used to support the greater good.

- Practice generosity now, even before you receive more—this shows you're ready to be a trustworthy steward.

- Stay sensitive to divine guidance; sometimes abundance is given in forms we don't expect but deeply need.

Mindfulness Practice:

1. Each week, prayerfully ask: *"How can I be a blessing with what I already have?"*

2. Then choose one specific way to give—whether your time, skills, encouragement, or resources—with no expectation of return.

3. Watch how your capacity to receive multiplies!

Final Thought:

We are not owners but stewards of abundance. *When we receive with open hands and open hearts, ready to give and serve, we enter the divine flow of provision. Abundance given for the greater good brings joy to others, glory to God, and true fulfillment to our souls.*

Law of Financial Health #6:
The Law of Righteousness and Wisdom

Principle:
"Attracting abundance comes from the application of Righteousness (which is right-doing) and Wisdom."

Righteous living is vital to your **prosperity** and God's word is what you do need to renew the mind. It is also what gives you the **wisdom**, knowledge and understanding, into how to be prosperous in everything that you do.!

The wisest man, King Solomon wrote, "Whoever pursues righteousness and love finds life, prosperity and honor." (Proverbs 21:21) This reveals that whatever you do, if your heart is in it and you do it with real love (which is selfless) and if it is done with the integrity of a righteous heart, you will be blessed in life and prosper and be honored and admired by others. He also spoke of wisdom (which is considered the very first Divine attribute that God manifested) saying, "Long life is in her right hand; In her left hand are riches and honor." So here Wisdom is described as both the source of longevity (health) and abundant wealth, and honor... showing that wisdom and righteousness are intricately woven together in that true wisdom will reveal itself in righteousness and true righteousness will reveal itself in wisdom, both leading to a long and prosperous life!

The **Law of Righteousness and Wisdom** teaches that lasting abundance flows through living with integrity and applying divine wisdom in all areas of life. **Righteousness**, or right-doing, is about aligning your actions with God's moral and ethical standards—doing what is just, honest, and loving. **Wisdom** is the ability to discern what is right and to make sound decisions that bring peace, prosperity, and purpose.

Together, righteousness and wisdom create a foundation that attracts abundance in a way that honors God and benefits others. When we live uprightly and act wisely, we become trustworthy stewards of resources, relationships, and influence.

How This Law Attracts Abundance:
Abundance is not simply about gaining more—**it's about becoming the kind of person who can be entrusted with more.** When we walk in righteousness and make wise, Spirit-led choices, we position ourselves under God's favor. Resources flow to those who will use them well—for good, not greed; for service, not selfishness.

Application:

How to Apply This Law Righteousness and Wisdom to attract Abundance…

- Let righteousness guide your daily choices—choose honesty, kindness, and integrity even when it costs something.

- Seek divine wisdom through prayer, Scripture, and wise counsel before making important financial or life decisions.

- Ask not just "Is this good for me?" but "Is this good for others? Does it honor God?"

- Align your financial goals and habits with principles that reflect justice, stewardship, and generosity.

Mindfulness Practice:

1. Each morning, pray for both righteousness and wisdom.

2. Then choose one area—relationships, finances, time management, or decision-making—and

3. Ask: *What is the right thing to do, and what is the wise way to do it?* Take one action that reflects both.

Final Thought:

Abundance rooted in righteousness and guided by wisdom is abundance that lasts. It not only blesses your life but becomes a river of blessing to others. When you walk uprightly and make choices anchored in truth, you attract not only provision, but peace, purpose, and divine favor.

Law of Financial Health #7:
The Law of Gratitude

Principle:
"Being thankful for not only what you have but also what you don't have yet is a powerful principle to believing it is coming and thereby manifesting it!"

We must give the Divine Source the glory for all things in gratitude and this is the reason why so many spiritual paths have prayers of gratitude and blessings proclaiming thanks for not only the things we have received but also for the things that we are about to receive!

For instance in Judaism there is a principle taken from the Torah in Deuteronomy 8:10 that instructs everyone to give thanks after they have eaten and are satisfied for the good land of a future inheritance which will produce much more food and blessings in the future. This also establishes the principle that reminds us it is so easy to forget God as the source of our blessings when we "are full" in other words when we are in need of nothing we tend to be full of ourselves and forget God and it is this time that it is most important to remember him as the source of all our blessings past present and future!

The **Law of Gratitude** teaches that a thankful heart is a magnet for abundance. Gratitude is more than polite manners—it's a spiritual force that aligns your heart with the flow of provision. When you give thanks not only for what you *already* have but also for what you *believe* is on the way, you express deep faith in divine timing and provision. This mindset invites more blessings into your life because it shows you're ready to receive and steward them well.

On the quantum level, gratitude shifts your vibrational frequency into alignment with abundance. When you feel genuine thankfulness, your heart and mind emit coherent, harmonious energy patterns that act like a magnetic signature, signaling the quantum field that you are already in possession of blessings.

This state of "already having" attracts matching frequencies, drawing more opportunities, resources, and blessings into your experience. Gratitude doesn't just acknowledge what is—it opens the door for more to flow in, because the universe mirrors the vibration you consistently radiate.

How Gratitude Attracts Wealth and Abundance:

Gratitude shifts your focus from lack to sufficiency. It tells the universe—and more importantly, your spirit—that you trust the Source of all resource. When you are thankful in advance, you activate a powerful belief that what you need is already on its way. And when that gratitude is rooted not just in personal desire but in a desire to bless others, it multiplies the impact of what you receive.

Application:

How to Apply This Law of Gratitude in Your Life to Attract Abundance...

- Begin and end each day by naming things you're grateful for—both visible blessings and unseen promises.
- When facing lack or delay, speak words of gratitude as if the answer has already come.
- Use gratitude as a way to refocus your intentions: not just "What can I get?" but "How can I give from what I have?"
- Practice thankfulness in your giving, knowing that what you release with a grateful heart returns in abundance.

Mindfulness Practice:

Keep a **Gratitude & Faith Journal**. Each day, write down:

1. Three things you're thankful for that you *already* have.
2. Three things you're thankful for that you *don't yet see*, but believe are coming—especially those that will enable you to serve others.
Let this journal become your spiritual record of faith and future harvest.

Final Thought:

Gratitude is the soil where abundance grows. When you live in thankfulness—both for the now and the not-yet—you align your heart with divine provision. And when your gratitude is not just for yourself but for what you can give, share, and do for others, you become a vessel through which true, lasting abundance flows.

Chapter Summary/Key Takeaways

In summary, these 7 laws work together to build a life of **financial health and abundance rooted in faith, purpose, and generosity.** When practiced in harmony, they not only attract wealth but help you become a channel of lasting abundance for the world around you!

In Overview, the 7 Laws of Financial Health and Abundance are...

1) **The Law of Oneness** with the Source of All Resource
Recognize that all abundance flows from one infinite Source—God. When you understand your connection to this Source and see yourself as a vessel for Divine provision, you open the way for abundance to flow to and through you for the greater good.

2) **The Law of Thinking, Believing & Feeling**
   Your thoughts, beliefs, and emotions shape your reality. To attract abundance, you must think positively, believe deeply, and feel with certainty that what you desire is already yours. This internal alignment magnetizes your external world.

3) **The Law of Only Speaking Good into Existence**
   Words carry creative power. Speak only what you desire to manifest—words of life, blessing, faith, and abundance. Reject negative speech and use your voice to declare purpose, prosperity, and goodness for yourself and others.

4) **The Law of Action**
   Faith must be followed by aligned action. Thinking and speaking positively must lead to consistent, intentional steps toward your vision. Taking action confirms your belief and activates the manifestation of abundance.

5) **The Law of Receiving Abundance for the Greater Good**
   Abundance is not meant for self-centered gain, but for shared impact. True financial health comes when your desire to receive is matched by your willingness to serve, give, and uplift others in alignment with God's will.

6) **The Law of Righteousness and Wisdom**
   Abundance flows through integrity and wise decision-making. Righteousness (right-doing) and divine wisdom guide you to use resources justly, make sound choices, and build wealth that honors God and benefits others.

7) **The Law of Gratitude**
   Gratitude is the key to unlocking and sustaining abundance. Be thankful for what you have and for what you believe is coming. Gratitude turns your heart toward faith, positions you to receive more, and multiplies what you're given.

Coming Up Next...

Now that we've explored the 7 Laws of Financial Health and Abundance, which guide us in aligning our mindset, words, actions, and intentions with divine prosperity, we can begin to see that abundance is part of a much larger, universal design. Beneath our interactions and experiences lies a divine order: the 7 Universal Laws.

These are not just abstract ideas, but spiritual principles that shape the very fabric of reality. They operate constantly in the invisible realm, influencing our thoughts, emotions, circumstances, and outcomes—whether we are aware of them or not. When we begin to understand and align with these universal laws, we gain the ability to live with greater harmony, purpose, and spiritual authority.

To deepen this understanding, we now turn our attention in the next chapter to the **7 Universal Laws of the Invisible Realm**—the foundational principles that govern all aspects of life, creation, and spiritual growth. These timeless truths offer a framework for living in harmony with the universe and with the Creator, helping us manifest a life of balance, purpose, and fulfillment beyond material gain.

Let's now explore these universal laws and discover how they interconnect with spiritual abundance, personal transformation, and the greater good!

CHAPTER SEVEN:
The 7 Universal Laws of the Invisible Realm

Beneath the surface of the physical world lies an invisible, spiritual realm governed by timeless principles—**the 7 Universal Laws**. These laws are not man-made doctrines or fleeting philosophies; they are Divine patterns woven into the very fabric of creation. Whether we are aware of them or not, they are always at work—shaping outcomes, influencing our experiences, and guiding the rhythm of life.

Rooted in ancient wisdom and spiritual truth, these Universal Laws reveal the order and intelligence behind all things. They help us understand how thoughts become reality, how opposites work in harmony, and how every action carries consequence. When we come into alignment with these laws, we move from struggle to flow, from confusion to clarity, and from separation to unity with both **nature and the Creator**.

By learning and honoring these Universal Laws, we awaken to the deeper realities of life and begin to cooperate with divine order rather than resist it. This alignment leads to greater peace, purpose, and power—not just for ourselves, but for the good of all creation.

Understanding the full spectrum of Universal Laws is like learning the complete blueprint for how life operates. Each law—whether it governs energy, relationships, health, or abundance—interacts with the others, creating a web of cause and effect on both the physical and quantum levels.

When we understand these principles, we stop living by accident and start living on purpose. We can align our thoughts, actions, and intentions with the natural flow of the universe, reducing resistance, avoiding unnecessary struggle, and accelerating growth. In essence, knowing the laws gives us the wisdom to work *with* the current rather than against it.

As you journey through each law, may you gain insight, deepen your connection with God, and find yourself more fully in tune with the sacred rhythm of the universe!

Universal Law #1:
The Law of Mentalism - "All is Mind"

Principle:
"All is Mind" is the substantial reality that underlies all the outward manifestations and appearances known as the material universe.

The **Law of Mentalism** is the first of the 7 Universal Laws and the foundation upon which all the others rest. It states that **"All is Mind"**—that everything we see, experience, and interact with in the physical world originates in a higher, unseen, intelligent Mind. This Divine Mind (God) is the **source and substance** of all that exists.

This law teaches us that the universe is not merely mechanical or material, but **spiritual and mental in nature**. The material world is a projection, a reflection of invisible mental energy. Our own minds are individualized expressions of the Universal Mind, meaning we are active participants in the shaping of our reality through our thoughts, beliefs, and consciousness.

On the quantum level, the Law of Mentalism reveals that **consciousness is the fundamental substance from which all reality emerges**. Instead of matter being the base, quantum physics shows that the universe is a vast field of probabilities shaped by observation, intention, and awareness—essentially, by mind.

The phrase, "All is Mind" means that the material universe, with all its forms and phenomena, is a **manifestation of underlying mental energy**—a dynamic, creative field of consciousness that gives rise to the physical world. What we perceive as solid and separate is actually a projection or expression of this universal mind, continuously shaped by collective and individual awareness.

Thus, the Law of Mentalism teaches us that by mastering our own mind—our thoughts, beliefs, and focus—we influence the very fabric of reality itself.

Application:

How to Apply this Law of Mentalism in Your Life for Greater Wellbeing...

- Recognize that your thoughts carry creative power—what you continually think about and focus on becomes your experience.

- Discipline your mind by replacing limiting thoughts with empowering, life-affirming ones rooted in truth and love.

- Align your thoughts with God's thoughts—pure, noble, wise, and loving—to manifest a life of harmony and peace.

- Understand that your inner world (beliefs, perceptions, and mental focus) must change before your outer world can.

Mindfulness Practice:

Each morning, **set your mental intention** for the day by affirming: "My mind is one with Divine Mind. I choose thoughts of peace, purpose, and prosperity. I think on what is true, and I manifest what is good."

Then, throughout the day, notice and gently correct any thoughts that contradict this mindset. Over time, your mental atmosphere will become fertile ground for wellbeing and abundance.

Final Thought:

*When you **understand that all is Mind**, you begin to take responsibility for your inner life, knowing it holds the power to shape your outer world. As you align your thoughts with the Divine, you step into the role of conscious co-creator—inviting peace, purpose, and abundance into every area of your life.*

Universal Law #2:
The Law of Correspondence

Principle:
"as above, so below; as within, so without."

The **Law of Correspondence** reveals the powerful truth that **"As above, so below; as within, so without."** This universal law teaches us that there is a constant reflection and harmony between the different levels of existence—spiritual and physical, mental and material, internal and external. What we experience on the outside is a mirror of what is happening on the inside.

Our relationships, environments, habits, and even the conditions of our lives are outward expressions of our inner world—our thoughts, emotions, beliefs, and spiritual alignment. To change our external reality, we must first address and transform our inner state.

On the quantum level, the Law of Correspondence shows that **the patterns we observe in the outer world are direct reflections of the patterns within consciousness.** Just as quantum particles respond to the expectations and focus of the observer, reality itself acts as a mirror, projecting outward the vibrational state of our inner thoughts, beliefs, and emotions.

The principle "as within, so without" plays out in quantum fields where **energy and information are entangled**, meaning the inner state of mind shapes the probability patterns that manifest in physical form. What we see is not an independent, fixed reality—it is **our consciousness translated into experience**, reflecting back to us the harmony or disharmony we hold within.

Application:

How to Apply This Law of Correspondence in Your Life for Greater Wellbeing...

- Examine areas of your life where there is struggle, confusion, or lack. Ask: *"What is this reflecting back to me about my inner thoughts or beliefs?"*
- Instead of only trying to fix external problems, focus on healing the root causes within—such as fear, limiting beliefs, or unforgiveness.
- Cultivate an inner environment of peace, clarity, faith, and gratitude. As your inner world shifts, your outer circumstances will begin to align.
- Trust that the visible world responds to the invisible truths you hold in your heart and mind.

Mindfulness Practice:

Start a **"Mirror Check-In"** journal.

1. Each day, write about one situation in your outer world (a relationship, financial issue, health, etc.) and,

2. Ask yourself:
   What does this reflect about my inner state?
   What thought, belief, or feeling might I need to shift?

3. Then write a positive inner affirmation or action step you can take to bring inner healing or alignment.

Final Thought:

The Law of Correspondence reminds us that we are not victims of life— we are reflections of it. When you take responsibility for your inner world and choose to nurture truth, peace, and purpose within, your outer world begins to respond with greater harmony, clarity, and abundance.

Universal Law #3:
The Law of Vibration

Principle:
"Nothing rests; everything moves; everything vibrates!"

The **Law of Vibration** states that **"nothing rests; everything moves; everything vibrates."** At the most fundamental level, everything in existence is energy in motion—even things that appear solid. Every thought, emotion, word, and object has a specific vibrational frequency. Since we live in a universe governed by energy and frequency, our personal vibration affects everything we attract and experience.

This law works in harmony with the **Law of Mentalism**, which reveals that all is Mind. Because every thought and feeling is a frequency, the quality of your internal vibration influences the quality of your external reality. **Low vibrations** such as fear, anger, and despair attract more of the same, while **high vibrations** like love, gratitude, peace, and joy produce harmony, health, and abundance.

On a quantum level, when your personal frequency aligns with the vibration of what you desire, quantum resonance increases the probability of that reality materializing in your experience. **Like frequencies attract and amplify each other**, meaning that raising your inner vibration through love, gratitude, and clarity directly shifts the energetic patterns that shape your physical world.

Thus, because everything is Mind;, everything is frequency... and healthy frequencies produce healthy results!

Application:

How to Apply This Law of Vibration in Your Life for Greater Wellbeing...

- Become aware of your emotional and mental states—your vibration is not just what you say or do, but what you consistently *feel and believe.*

- Surround yourself with uplifting environments, people, music, and content that elevate your frequency.

- Raise your vibration through prayer, meditation, praise, movement, kindness, gratitude, and intentional thought.

- Speak life-giving words, as sound and speech are vibrational forces that either heal or harm.

- Choose foods, thoughts, and habits that carry life-enhancing energy.

Mindfulness Practice:

Begin each day with a **Vibration-Setting Ritual:**

1. Sit quietly and breathe deeply.

2. Speak aloud an affirmation such as: *"I align my thoughts, emotions, and actions with the highest frequencies of love, peace, and divine purpose."*

3. Listen to uplifting music, stretch, or spend a few minutes in gratitude to raise your energetic state.
   Repeat this throughout the day whenever your energy feels low or scattered.

Final Thought:

Your vibration is your spiritual signature—it tells the universe what you're ready to receive. When you consciously align your thoughts, emotions, and choices with high frequencies, you don't just change your mood—you change your life. By raising your vibration, you come into harmony with divine intelligence and attract what is whole, good, and life-giving.

Universal Law #4:
The Law of Polarity

Principle
"Everything can be seen having an opposite; and yet opposites are identical in nature yet different in degree. All paradoxes may be thus reconciled."

The **Law of Polarity** teaches that **everything has its opposite**—and yet those opposites are not in conflict, but **two extremes of the same essence**. Light and darkness, hot and cold, joy and sorrow, abundance and lack—each are different in degree, but not in kind. This law reveals that **all paradoxes can be reconciled** when we understand the reality of their deeper unity.

On the quantum level, the Law of Polarity shows that **everything exists in complementary pairs part of a greater whole**—positive and negative charges, matter and antimatter, wave and particle—each defining and balancing the other. Just as the macrocosm of the universe holds galaxies and voids in equilibrium, the microcosm of subatomic particles depends on polar forces to create structure, motion, and stability. Without contrast, there is no perception, growth, or creation. Recognizing this polarity in life and relationships allows us to see challenges as necessary counterpoints to blessings, creating a dynamic harmony that sustains both the physical and spiritual realms.

At the spiritual level, polarity exists to help us grow in wisdom and balance. Without darkness, light has no meaning; without sadness, joy cannot be fully appreciated. Polarity is not punishment—it's part of a divine design to refine our awareness and help us choose alignment with the higher end of any spectrum.

Application:

How to Apply This Law of Polarity in Your Life for Greater Wellbeing...

- When facing a challenge, shift your perspective: ask, *"What is the opposite of this experience? How can I begin to move toward it?"*
- Understand that no emotional or situational state is fixed—you can choose to elevate your vibration and move from fear to faith, from despair to hope, from scarcity to abundance.
- Learn to see contrast as a tool for clarity. The presence of what you don't want helps define and refine what you do want.
- Don't resist life's lows—instead, use them as leverage to climb toward the highs with greater wisdom and empathy.

Mindfulness Practice:

Try a **Polarity Reframing** Exercise:

1. Identify one negative emotion or situation you're experiencing.
2. Write down its opposite (e.g., fear to courage, confusion to clarity).
3. Reflect or journal: *"What thoughts, beliefs, or actions would move me closer to this higher state?"*
4. Take one small step in that direction—mentally, emotionally, or practically.

Final Thought:

The Law of Polarity reminds us that we are never stuck—we are simply on a spectrum, and we always have the power to shift. Every low point holds the seed of its opposite. **As we grow in awareness and alignment with the divine, we learn to rise above extremes and live from a place of centered peace, knowing that both shadow and light serve a greater purpose in the unfolding of our abundant life.**

Universal Law #5:
The Law of Rhythm

Principle:
"Everything flows, out an in like tides; All things rise and fall – All rhythm compensates"

The **Law of Rhythm** teaches that **everything in the universe flows in cycles**—a continuous movement of rising and falling, expansion and contraction, forward motion and retreat. Like the tides of the sea, the phases of the moon, the seasons of nature, and the beat of the heart, **all things are subject to rhythm**. This law reveals that there is divine order even in what appears to be change, chaos, or uncertainty.

On the quantum level, this law is seen in the **natural cycles and oscillations** that govern all matter and energy—electrons orbiting nuclei, photons pulsing as waves, and cosmic patterns unfolding in predictable beats. Every particle vibrates in rhythmic motion, creating seasons of expansion and contraction, activity and rest. This ebb and flow maintains balance and ensures continual renewal. When we align with these rhythms in our own lives—embracing both highs and lows—we harmonize with the same quantum pulse that keeps the universe in motion.

The Law of Rhythm also reveals that **"All rhythm compensates"**—meaning that what swings to one side must eventually swing to the other. When we experience a high, a corresponding low will follow. But this is not to be feared. It's a **natural balancing force** that keeps life evolving, stretching us, grounding us, and teaching us to flow rather than resist.

Applying this awareness in life allows us to ride challenges like waves rather than be overcome by them, promoting greater balance, resilience, and wellbeing in body, mind, and spirit.

Application:

How to Apply This Law in Your Life for Greater Wellbeing:

- Recognize that **no state is permanent**—neither joy nor sorrow, abundance nor lack, energy nor fatigue. Learn to accept all situations as manifestations of change and move with the rhythm embracing it for your good rather than fighting against it.
- During high seasons, cultivate gratitude and humility. In low seasons, practice patience, self-care, and faith that the tide will rise again.
- Use rhythmic awareness to pace yourself—spiritually, emotionally, and practically—honoring the seasons of both activity and rest.
- Trust that even in stillness or delay, movement is happening beneath the surface.

Mindfulness Practice:

Try a **"Rhythm Awareness Reflection"** at the end of each week:

1. Reflect on the emotional, spiritual, and physical rhythms you experienced.
2. Identify one area where you felt "in the flow" and one where you resisted.
3. Ask: *"How can I better honor the rhythm in this area next week?"*
4. Set one intention that supports flow—like resting more, praying in quiet, or slowing down your pace.

Final Thought:

*The Law of Rhythm invites us to **live with grace, patience, and trust**. Life is not meant to be a constant high or uninterrupted success. It moves in waves and seasons, just as God designed. When you embrace this divine rhythm, you move through life with more peace and resilience—dancing with the flow rather than being swept away by it.*

Universal Law #6:
The Law of Cause and Effect

Principle:
"Every cause has an effect and every effect has a cause. Everything happens according to law. Chance, luck and miracles are but names for laws not recognized.

The **Law of Cause and Effect** teaches that **nothing happens by chance—every action has a corresponding reaction.** Every thought, word, emotion, and behavior sends out a ripple into the universe, and that ripple eventually returns, often multiplied. This law is rooted in the divine order and intelligence that governs the universe. What may appear random is actually governed by unseen spiritual laws at work.

This law reveals that we are not victims of life's circumstances, but co-creators of our experiences. Whether in health, relationships, finances, or spiritual growth, the results we experience today are the effects of causes we (or others) have set into motion—consciously or unconsciously.

And This is why we do not say we are lucky or that things happen according to chance but we understand either we are blessed by living in harmony with invisible law or we lose those blessings when we live contrary to the law of selfless love in all its forms.

On the quantum level, energy cannot move without influencing the field around it. Just as subatomic particles respond instantly to forces and inputs, our intentions, choices, and behaviors ripple outward, shaping the reality we experience. By becoming conscious of the "causes" we set in motion—through our thinking, speech, and actions—we can deliberately generate positive effects, leading to greater harmony, health, and fulfillment in our lives!

Application:

How to Apply This Law in Your Life for Greater Wellbeing:

- Take full responsibility for your life—both the blessings and the challenges—knowing they are connected to seeds (causes) planted through thought, choice, or belief.

- Make intentional choices that align with truth, love, and righteousness, understanding that those causes will bear good fruit.

- Avoid blame or self-condemnation; instead, become conscious of your power to change your future by changing the causes you're sowing now.

- Trust that when you do good, even if unseen for a season, the effects will come in divine timing.

Mindfulness Practice:

Start a **Cause-and-Effect Tracker** for a week. Each evening, reflect on:

1. One positive thing you experienced today—trace it back to a choice, thought, or action that led to it.

2. One negative or challenging moment—ask yourself gently: *"What cause might I have planted?"*
   Then, prayerfully ask what seed you can plant tomorrow for a better harvest—such as kindness, forgiveness, discipline, or gratitude.

Final Thought:

The Law of Cause and Effect reminds us that **life is not happening to us—it is responding to us.** *Every seed matters. Every thought matters. And every loving action sown in faith will produce fruit in time. Live with awareness, plant wisely, and you will align with the divine flow of wellbeing, purpose, and abundance.*

Universal Law #7:
The Law of Gender

Principle:
"Gender is in everything – Male and Female manifests on all levels."

The **Law of Gender** teaches that **both masculine and feminine principles exist in all things and on all levels—spiritual, mental, and physical.** It is not limited to biological sex, but is a deeper universal truth about balance, creation, and manifestation. Just as nature requires both seed and soil to bring forth life, **so too do our thoughts, intentions, and actions require both masculine and feminine energies to be fruitful.**

- The **masculine** energy is active, initiating, logical, and outward-moving.
- The **feminine** energy is receptive, intuitive, nurturing, and inward-moving.

Together, they reflect the image of the Creator and are essential to the process of birth, growth, and transformation in every area of life. When these energies are in harmony within us, we live with greater creativity, wisdom, and power.

The Interplay of the Law of Gender and the Law of Polarity: The Dance of Creation...

The **Law of Gender** and the **Law of Polarity** are intimately connected, working together to uphold the balance and rhythm of the universe. These two laws reflect divine principles woven into all levels of existence—from the structure of atoms to the mysteries of spiritual creation.

At the **energetic level**, we see this union expressed through **positive and negative charges**, particularly in the behavior of electrons and protons. Every atom—the basic building block of the universe—is held together by this sacred polarity. **Positive and negative charges do not conflict; they attract and stabilize.** This is not a struggle, but a dance. Their union produces structure, harmony, and the capacity for life to exist and continually **recreate itself.**

This mirrors the **Law of Gender**, where the **masculine (active, initiating)** and **feminine (receptive, nurturing)** energies co-create all that exists. The masculine is not superior, nor is the feminine lesser—they are **equal and complementary**, each essential to creation and rebirth.

In human consciousness, these laws exists as well:

- The **mind is the seed of conception** (masculine),
- The **heart nurtures and births** (feminine),
- And together, they manifest thought into form.

  **Without polarity, there would be no movement.
  Without gender, there would be no creation.**

This Also Applies Spiritually and Practically:

- When you learn to **honor both the active and receptive forces** within and around you, you come into alignment with how life was designed to function.
- Your ideas (masculine) must be given stillness, intuition, and nurturing (feminine) to develop and become reality.
- Every challenge (negative pole) holds a solution (positive pole); every ending (feminine) leads to a new beginning (masculine).

- When you feel off-balance, ask: *"Am I honoring both energies within me, or resisting one?"*

Thus Creation is not a one-time event—it is constant. The polarity of energies and the gendered forces within the universe ensure that life is always evolving, growing, and re-creating itself.

We are part of that flow and by understanding and integrating these energies within ourselves, we align with the natural creative process of the universe, allowing our endeavors, relationships, and personal growth to flourish in harmony!

Application:

How to Apply This Law in Your Life for Greater Wellbeing:
- Cultivate **balance** in your life. Are you constantly "doing" without reflection? That's an overuse of masculine energy. Or are you stuck in passivity or overthinking? That may be an overuse of feminine energy.
- Make space for **both action and intuition, logic and emotion, giving and receiving**.
- In decision-making, **receive inner guidance (feminine), then take focused steps (masculine)** to bring that insight into reality.
- In relationships and work, honor the unique strengths that both energies bring without diminishing one or the other.

Mindfulness Practice:

Try a Daily *"Gender Balance Check-In"*:

1. In the morning, set your intention: "Today, I honor both the active and receptive parts of myself."

2. In the evening, ask:
   - Did I take courageous action today? (Masculine)
   - Did I create space to reflect, listen, rest or receive? (Feminine)

3. Note where you felt imbalanced and adjust tomorrow to bring greater harmony.

Final Thought:

The Law of Gender reminds us that **true power comes not from dominance, but from balance.** *When the masculine and feminine energies within us walk together in unity, we become aligned with divine order—able to create, nurture, and manifest not only for ourselves, but for the good of all. In this sacred balance, abundance flows naturally and life flourishes.*

Chapter Summary/Key Takeaways

In summary, if your mind can conceive it, you can achieve it! The 7 Universal Laws are:

1. **The Law of Mentalism** – All is Divine Consciousness and originates in the mind of God and flows through consciousness. We are an extension of that Universal consciousness, thus, what we hold in thought shapes our reality.

2. **The Law of Correspondence** – "As above, so below; as within, so without." Our outer world reflects our inner state, and our individual life mirrors spiritual truth.

3. **The Law of Vibration** – Everything is energy in motion. What we vibrate—through thoughts, emotions, and beliefs—we attract into our lives.

4. **The Law of Polarity** – Everything has its opposite. Light and dark, joy and sorrow, wealth and lack are two ends of the same spectrum. Understanding this helps us find balance and perspective.

5. **The Law of Rhythm** – Life moves in cycles and seasons. There is a natural ebb and flow to all things. Trusting the rhythm brings peace in both the highs and the lows.

6. **The Law of Cause and Effect** – Every action creates a reaction. Nothing happens by chance. When we take intentional, righteous action, we set in motion positive outcomes.

7. **The Law of Gender** – All creation contains both masculine and feminine energy—logic and intuition, action and nurture. Harmony comes when these forces are balanced within and expressed outwardly.

Well Done! You've just taken a powerful and courageous step — not just by reading this book, but by opening yourself to a life of intentional growth, healing, and lasting transformation. You now hold within you the understanding of **7 eternal Laws** that operate across **every area of life** — from your thoughts and emotions to your health, relationships, finances, work, and spiritual understanding!

These aren't just ideas. These are **unchanging principles** woven into the fabric of creation — Laws that, when honored and applied daily, open the door to the very blessings God designed you to experience: **peace, clarity, joy, purpose, abundance, and wholeness!**

Epilogue/Conclusion

A Life Transformed by Divine Law

Congratulations! You have journeyed through a sacred exploration—one that has revealed how every area of your life is governed by **divine, invisible laws** designed for your good. You've uncovered **seven realms of life**, each woven together by **seven foundational laws**, making **forty-nine timeless principles** that shape your Divine identity, your connection to Creative consciousness, your emotions, your relationships, your health, your wealth, your purpose, and your peace!

These laws are not man-made rules or religious constraints—they are **spiritual blueprints**, embedded in the fabric of creation by the Source of all life. They are not meant to control you, but **to free you once you understand them and live by them**. They are not meant to burden you, but to **bless you**. When honored, they do not just help you survive—they empower you to **thrive, rise, and live a transcendent life!**

You now carry the keys to:

- *Spiritual elevation through oneness with the Divine.*
- *Health and Happiness through applying the laws of nature*
- *Abundance through spiritual alignment.*
- *Harmonious relationships through communication and truth.*
- *Peace and emotional balance through understanding vibration, polarity, and rhythm.*
- *Purposeful action and fulfillment through right-doing, wisdom, and gratitude.*
- *Creativity and manifestation through laws of Mental Mastery... and so much more!*

These laws do not operate only when we are aware of them—they are always in motion and always apply. But awareness is the key that gives you **the power to live intentionally**, to choose your responses, to align with divine order, and to become an agent of light, love, and life in a world hungry for truth.

The Invitation Forward

As you close this book, you are not ending a study—you are stepping into a **new way of being**. Apply what you've learned. Live it out with faith.

Return to this book and these principles often, share it with your family and friends and let these principles guide your choices, shape your mindset, and form the foundation of everything you do. You don't have to master all of them at once. Transformation is a rhythm, not a race. Keep your heart humble, your mind open, and your spirit willing—and you will see evidence of these laws manifesting in your life in powerful ways.

Final Word: The Transcendent Life Awaits

The Transcendent Life is not reserved for a chosen few—it is the destiny of every soul awakened to truth. It is a life lived in alignment with heaven's design. A life of flow instead of friction, of peace instead of striving, of grace instead of fear.

You were created for this. You are ready.

Now go forward with boldness, wisdom, and joy—**not just knowing the laws that govern life, but embodying them**—and experience the Divine beauty of a life lifted above limitation, anchored in truth, and overflowing with abundance for the good of all.

This is Transcendent Living!

Bibliography of Foundational Texts and Spiritual Principles

The following sources represent the ancient, scriptural, and philosophical foundations upon which the universal and spiritual laws presented in this book are based. These texts have influenced countless traditions, offering timeless insight into the nature of abundance, balance, wisdom, right action, and divine alignment.

Ancient Spiritual Teachers:

Hermes Trismegistus. (n.d.). *The Kybalion: A Study of the Hermetic Philosophy of Ancient Egypt and Greece* (The Three Initiates, Trans.). Yogi Publication Society.
An early 20th-century distillation of Hermetic teachings attributed to Hermes Trismegistus, exploring the seven Hermetic laws including mentalism, correspondence, vibration, polarity, rhythm, cause and effect, and gender.
Solomon, King of Israel. (950 BCE). *The Book of Proverbs* and *Ecclesiastes*. In *The Holy Bible* (Various translations).
Wisdom literature emphasizing righteousness, cause and effect, gratitude, right speech, and divine understanding.
Moses. (13th Century BCE.). *The Torah / Pentateuch (Genesis–Deuteronomy)*. In *The Holy Bible* (Various translations).
The foundational moral and spiritual laws of the Hebrew Scriptures, including sowing and reaping, obedience, divine justice, and covenant principles.
Yeshua. (Jesus of Nazareth). (n.d.). *The Gospels (Matthew–John)*. In *The Holy Bible* (Various translations).
Teachings on inner transformation, the kingdom of God, gratitude, abundant life, faith, right action, and spiritual law.
Lao Tzu. (6th Century BCE). *Tao Te Ching* (S. Mitchell, Trans., 1988). HarperPerennial.

An ancient Chinese text describing universal harmony, flow, polarity, humility, and living in balance with the Tao (the Way).

The Bhagavad Gita. (2004). (E. Easwaran, Trans.). Nilgiri Press.
A sacred Hindu scripture that presents teachings on karma (cause and effect), dharma (righteous action), detachment, devotion, and spiritual duty.

The Dhammapada (Teachings of the Buddha). (1985). (E. Easwaran, Trans.). Nilgiri Press.
A Buddhist text presenting moral and mental laws, including the power of thoughts, right speech, mindfulness, and compassion.

Plato. (c. 380 BCE). *The Republic* (B. Jowett, Trans.). Oxford University Press.
A classical Greek philosophical dialogue exploring justice, inner harmony, the world of forms, and the role of wisdom and truth in society.

Plotinus. (c. 270 CE). *The Enneads* (S. MacKenna, Trans., 1991). Penguin Classics.
A foundational work of Neoplatonism exploring the soul's connection to the Divine (the One), and how spiritual ascent is governed by metaphysical law.

Note to Readers:
While not all of these texts use the exact modern terminology of "laws of abundance," "vibration," or "universal principles," the spiritual truths they present are the **roots of these understandings.** *This bibliography serves as a bridge between ancient wisdom and modern application, honoring the divine pattern present in all of creation.*

Bibliography of Jewish Wisdom and Talmudic Teachings

This bibliography highlights foundational Jewish sources—ancient, medieval, and modern—that explore the divine structure of the universe, moral and spiritual laws, and the transformative power of thought, word, deed, and intention. These teachings are embedded deeply in Torah, Talmud, and the mystical tradition, affirming the spiritual principles presented throughout this book.

Foundational Texts and Rabbinic Commentary

The Holy Scriptures. (n.d.). *Tanakh (Torah, Nevi'im, Ketuvim).* Jewish Publication Society.

The Hebrew Bible is the cornerstone of Jewish spiritual law and wisdom, encompassing divine principles such as righteousness (tzedek), justice (mishpat), mercy (chesed), and abundance through alignment with God's will.

The Talmud Bavli. (Various Rabbis & Sages). (n.d.). (Soncino Edition, I. Epstein, Ed.). Soncino Press.

A vast compilation of rabbinical discussions on Jewish law, ethics, philosophy, and customs. Contains extensive insights on cause and effect (middah k'neged middah), the power of speech (lashon hara vs. lashon tov), and spiritual balance.

Maimonides (Rambam). (1190). *The Guide for the Perplexed* (M. Friedländer, Trans., 1904). Dover Publications.

A foundational philosophical work bridging Jewish theology with rational metaphysics. Maimonides explores divine wisdom, creation, and moral alignment with God's will.

Nachmanides (Ramban). (c. 13th century). *Commentary on the Torah.* Mossad HaRav Kook.

Provides mystical and ethical interpretations of the Torah, emphasizing divine providence, balance, and the spiritual structure of the world.

Rabbi Moshe Chaim Luzzatto (Ramchal). (1734). *The Path of the Just (Mesillat Yesharim)* (M. Kaplan, Trans., 1966). Feldheim Publishers.

A masterful ethical work outlining the path to spiritual refinement, including principles of intention, purity, humility, righteousness, and wisdom.

Rabbi Aryeh Kaplan. (1990). *Jewish Meditation: A Practical Guide.* Schocken Books.

Bridges traditional Jewish spirituality with inner disciplines such as thought awareness, focused speech, and energetic alignment with the Divine.

Rabbi Abraham Joshua Heschel. (1955). *God in Search of Man: A Philosophy of Judaism.* Farrar, Straus and Giroux.

A deeply spiritual and philosophical work discussing divine-human relationship, revelation, moral purpose, and sacred action.

Rabbi Menachem Mendel Schneerson (The Lubavitcher Rebbe). (1995). *Toward a Meaningful Life* (S. Jacobson, Ed.). William Morrow.

A contemporary spiritual synthesis of Chassidic teachings focused on living with purpose, abundance, divine service, and unity with God.

More Mystical Sources

Sefer Yetzirah (The Book of Formation). (c. 2nd century CE). (A. Kaplan, Trans., 1990). Weiser Books.

One of the oldest known Kabbalistic texts. Explores creation through letters, numbers, and spiritual laws including polarity, vibration, and divine emanations.

The Zohar. (13th century). *The Book of Splendor* (D. C. Matt, Trans., 2004). Stanford University Press.

The foundational text of Kabbalah, revealing esoteric insights into the nature of reality, divine attributes (Sefirot), spiritual law, and the interconnectedness of all things.

Rabbi Isaac Luria (The Ari). (c. 1570). *Etz Chaim (Tree of Life).* (Modern commentaries and translations available from various Kabbalistic centers.)

Outlines the spiritual dynamics of creation, contraction (tzimtzum), balance of male/female energy (Law of Gender), and divine cause and effect.

Rabbi Chaim Vital. (17th century). *Shaar HaGilgulim (Gates of Reincarnation).* (Translated selections available through Kabbalistic literature.)

A Kabbalistic exploration of soul correction, divine justice, and the cyclical rhythms of spiritual law across lifetimes.

Note to Readers:

The wisdom of the Torah and the Rabbis is not static—it is living, breathing, and continually illuminating new depths of understanding. The spiritual principles covered in this book resonate profoundly with Jewish teachings on divine order, moral law, soul refinement, and the ultimate unity between God, creation, and human purpose.

The following more modern sources also have made great contributions to helping others understand many of these same principles in Transcendent Living and whose writings reflect, articulate, or expand on the spiritual laws covered in this book. These authors have contributed significantly to the understanding and application of spiritual law, divine order, abundance, right thinking, and higher

More Modern Spiritual Teachers and Authors:

Allen, J. (1903). *As a Man Thinketh.* Thomas Y. Crowell & Co.
A concise but profound exploration of the power of thought to shape one's character, circumstances, and destiny.
Holmes, E. (1938). *The Science of Mind: A Philosophy, a Faith, a Way of Life.* Tarcher/Putnam.
A comprehensive spiritual system that unites metaphysics, psychology, and affirmative prayer to align with Divine Mind.
Hill, N. (1937). *Think and Grow Rich.* The Ralston Society.
A pioneering book in personal development and prosperity consciousness, grounded in principles of belief, desire, faith, and definite purpose.
Hall, M. P. (1928). *The Secret Teachings of All Ages.* Philosophical Research Society.
A scholarly and mystical survey of ancient wisdom traditions, symbols, alchemy, and esoteric philosophy.
Szekely, E. B. (Trans.). (1928). *The Essene gospel of peace: Book one.* International Biogenic Society.
Troward, T. (1915). *The Creative Process in the Individual.* Dodd, Mead & Co.
Explores how universal spiritual laws operate in consciousness and creativity, laying the foundation for New Thought philosophy.
Fox, E. (1932). *The Seven Main Aspects of God.* Unity School of Christianity.
A metaphysical look at divine law, attributes of God, and practical spirituality rooted in positive thinking and affirmation.

Butterworth, E. (1989). *Spiritual Economics: The Principles and Process of True Prosperity.* Unity House.
A metaphysical guide to prosperity consciousness, abundance, and aligning wealth with spiritual law and inner growth.
Murphy, J. (1963). *The Power of Your Subconscious Mind.* Prentice Hall.
An influential work on the relationship between belief, subconscious suggestion, and real-world manifestation.
Wattles, W. D. (1910). *The Science of Getting Rich.* Elizabeth Towne Company.
A practical treatise on wealth creation rooted in thought, gratitude, and alignment with the universal creative substance.
Baer, Greg (2018) Real love. *What is Real love?* Retrieved from https://www.reallove.com/what-is-real-love/

Note to Readers:
*This above references from ancient and modern texts reflects the **ongoing revelation of spiritual law** throughout human history. Whether articulated through sacred scripture, Eastern philosophy, or metaphysical science, the universal truths governing thought, energy, creation, and abundance remain timeless and relevant. These laws do not contradict one another—they harmonize across cultures and centuries, offering us a clear path toward transcendent, purposeful living.*

ABOUT THE AUTHOR

 Isaac Heckman is an international speaker, spiritual teacher, author, life strategist, humanitarian and healer and founder of *Transcendent Living Health and Wellness Centers* (www.transcendentliving.org). Isaac's life work has been dedicated to helping people heal, awaken to their divine identity and highest potential, and live more fulfilled, transcendent lives and has spent over 30 years facilitating this in many capacities around the world!

Isaac began his early work in psychology counseling at-risk youth for the State of Texas, applying many of the very principles found in this book with remarkable success. His philanthropic focus then expanded to worldwide humanitarian service in 1996 to help more children worldwide and in 2008 he founded *Serving Others Worldwide (www.servingothers.org)* —an international nonprofit devoted to "sowing seeds of love through service" establishing schools, building medical clinics, and helping widows and orphans in underprivileged communities while providing volunteer opportunities for others to experience the blessing of giving as well— and has combined his deep spiritual insights with hands-on action to transform lives across the globe.

In 2015 while furthering his spiritual studies in Israel, Isaac was called back to the United States to teach the timeless laws of Torah at the *Assembly of Called-Out Believers* (www.calledoutbelievers.org) which brought about over 200 spiritual video teachings uploaded on YouTube garnering millions of viewers and students worldwide, inspiring a modern day movement of sincere truth-seekers seeking to live out these timeless truths and inspiring this book!

As a counselor, teacher, and guide, Isaac has seen countless lives transformed through the eternal laws of love, kindness, and divine wisdom. With *Transcendent Living*, he shares these timeless principles with the world—offering every reader from every culture a clear path to God's design for health, joy, and abundant living!

www.ingramcontent.com/pod-product-compliance
Lightning Source LLC
Chambersburg PA
CBHW030449100526
44580CB00002B/52